It's Not
"One More Thing"

Control vs.
influence
CC mtg

It's Not "One More Thing"

Culturally Responsive and Affirming Strategies in K–12 Literacy Classrooms

Anne Swenson Ticknor,
Christy Howard, and Mikkaka Overstreet

ROWMAN & LITTLEFIELD
Lanham • Boulder • New York • London

Published by Rowman & Littlefield
An imprint of The Rowman & Littlefield Publishing Group, Inc.
4501 Forbes Boulevard, Suite 200, Lanham, Maryland 20706
www.rowman.com

6 Tinworth Street, London, SE11 5AL, United Kingdom

British Library Cataloguing in Publication Information Available

Library of Congress Cataloging-in-Publication Data

Names: Ticknor, Anne Swenson, 1973– author. | Howard, Christy, 1978– author. | Overstreet, Mikkaka, 1984– author.
Title: It's not "one more thing" : culturally responsive and affirming strategies in K–12 literacy classrooms / Anne Swenson Ticknor, Christy Howard, and Mikkaka Overstreet.
Description: Lanham : Rowman & Littlefield, 2021. | Includes bibliographical references and index. | Summary: "This book offers theoretical and practical applications for teacher educators, preservice teachers, and in-service teachers in culturally responsive pedagogy."— Provided by publisher.
Identifiers: LCCN 2021002097 (print) | LCCN 2021002098 (ebook) | ISBN 9781475857139 (cloth) | ISBN 9781475857146 (paperback) | ISBN 9781475857153 (epub)
Subjects: LCSH: English language—Study and teaching (Elementary)—Social aspects. | English language—Study and teaching (Secondary)—Social aspects. | Culturally relevant pedagogy.
Classification: LCC LB1576 .T53 2021 (print) | LCC LB1576 (ebook) | DDC 372.6—dc23
LC record available at https://lccn.loc.gov/2021002097
LC ebook record available at https://lccn.loc.gov/2021002098

We dedicate this book to all the teachers who affirm their students'
identities and lives in their classrooms and curriculums.

Education can't save us. We have to save education.

—Dr. Bettina Love

Contents

Acknowledgments

We acknowledge that this book would not be possible without the support of many people and communities in our individual and collective lives. We want to thank the community of teachers who have supported and taught us to be more culturally responsive teachers. We want to thank all of our students, both K–12 and college, who demanded that we affirm their lives in our teaching. We thank our fabulous graduate assistants, Ashley-Laren and Bethany, for their tireless assistance. We also thank Carlie and Nicole at Rowman & Littlefield for working with us throughout this process. Finally, we want to thank each other for all of the things.

Anne would like to thank her community of Las Vegas teachers, the Amigas (Ardrena, Cathy, Mery, Nancy, and Sarah), for their unwavering encouragement, urging, and feedback from her first day of teaching to now; her community of women faculty (the Lazy Bottoms and the Angels) who answered her questions about writing a book, provided space for writing at the beach, and toasted each success; and, most importantly, Rob, who always believes in and celebrates her.

Christy would like to thank her writing friends (Claire, Joy, and Melissa) for their consistent support and encouragement not only in the creation of this book but also in everything related to writing and life. Even though Melissa is no longer with us, she is always here with us. Christy thanks her sister scholars #WeGettingTenure (Loni, Janeè, and Mikkaka) for constantly being the light, laughter, and love in what can often be a very dark world. Special thanks to Maya for reading these chapters aloud when Christy needed to hear them from someone else and a special thank you to Jeremy for always believing she could do all the things and giving her time and space to do them.

Mikkaka is overwhelmed with gratitude. This book just feels so right, and that is thanks to all the teachers, students, families, preservice teachers, and other scholars she's learned with over the past 20 years. She thanks her mentors for their guidance and encouragement. Special thanks to #WeGettingTenure (Loni, Janeè, and Christy) for being such a supportive group of sister scholars. To her writing group (Monica, Africa, Ya-Huei, and Janet), thanks for keeping her motivated. And, of course, to her vampire for being her anchor, biggest cheerleader, and voice of reason, no matter what.

Introduction

I (Christy) teach an undergraduate course on literacy learning in a diverse world. This course focuses on home, school, and community literacy connections while valuing students' identities and funds of knowledge outside of the classroom. In this course, we discuss the importance of looking beyond the single story (Adichie, 2009) in the lives of students and in texts. We discuss the importance of providing mirrors and windows (Bishop, 1990) for students as they engage in reading, and we discuss the importance of being culturally responsive teachers. As a Black woman teaching this course to primarily white, middle-class women, I recognize that our worldviews and experiences may be different, and I always address this by doing identity work with my students; however, by the end of the third week of class this particular semester, I felt there was a disconnection between me and my students. I felt there was still a "coldness" in the room as I discussed the importance of validating the lived experiences of diverse students, and I couldn't figure out why. Finally, near the end of class, exasperated, I sat on my desk. "You all are always so quiet," I said. "Why don't you engage in discussions? Why don't you share your thoughts and ideas?" I looked around the classroom at wide eyes but silent mouths. Finally, a student raised her hand and shared, "This is all just new to me, and I'm trying to take it in. I've never had a [whisper] Black professor before, and before coming to school here, I was never in a class with Black students. It's a lot to take in when you're talking about diversity and having these students in my classroom." Other students began to chime in with similar experiences. Some students discussed how they planned to go back to their hometowns to teach and did not expect to encounter diversity, so they were unsure as to how they would use the knowledge gained in this course. We discussed what this meant for their understanding and experiences of diversity. During this class session, students began to open up and share their questions and concerns as I shared my personal experiences with them about being the only Black student in classrooms throughout most of my K–12 education. I shared with them how I wished I had teachers that saw me, valued me, and engaged me in a curriculum that was relevant to my life and my experiences. Leaving class that day, I was relieved, feeling we had broken a barrier of communication and started to build a classroom community, but I was also more discouraged about the idea that some students did not understand the importance of providing culturally relevant experiences for all students and, in addition, providing multiple perspectives from the lives of diverse students. I felt even more determined and invested in this work, not just for the students who look like me but also for the students who don't. I felt even more invested in showing the beauty of diverse experiences, cultures, interests, and so on and showing the connections between these identities and how students learn in classrooms.

We open with this scene from Christy's class to demonstrate the kinds of conversations we have with our preservice teachers (PSTs) and to illustrate the importance of teachers engaging in professional learning on culturally responsive teaching. America's teachers—who are predominantly white, middle-class, monolingual women (Bissonnette, 2016; National Center for Education Statistics, 2016)—are educating the most racially, ethnically, and linguistically diverse group of students in U.S. history (Darling-Hammond, 2008). America's K–12 students (and their families) represent many races, ethnicities, sexualities, abilities, gender identities, and cultures. Teachers of all backgrounds need to be prepared to effectively educate students of all backgrounds as well as to prepare students for a world in which they will encounter many people different from themselves.

Our intent in this book is not to critique our teacher colleagues in the field, and, as former classroom teachers, we are well aware of the complexities that lead to instructional decisions that aren't best for kids. We know how difficult it can be to enact our visions as teachers in ways that affirm and build on our students' lives outside of our classrooms and that many hurdles are almost impossible to overcome. We know that federal and district mandates can limit the materials we select for and use in our instruction. We also know that teachers are overworked and that finding new instructional resources to support a change in how we teach can require more time, money, and effort than we have. We also know about the real pressures of program fidelity and how high-stakes tests can limit our instructional time and decisions. And we also know that collaborative planning with our grade-level or content colleagues can provide added benefits to our instruction while at the same time limiting our individual teaching decisions. Our intent, then, is to offer this book as a part of the process for educators, recognizing that there is not one book or one idea that will drive this work but rather many pieces that will come together across different classrooms. We hope this book provides readers practical ways to integrate more equity-focused and culturally affirming pedagogies into their regular literacy instruction.

To do this, it is important to examine ourselves as educators (Ahmed, 2018a, 2018b; Souto-Manning, Llerena, Martell, Maguire, & Arce-Boardman, 2018) and critically reflect on our identities, beliefs, and experiences and how these components influence how we teach. If "what and how we read is mediated by our experiences" (Ryan & Hermann-Wilmarth, 2018, p. 9), we must examine and deconstruct our own experiences along with the experiences of our students in order to meet their diverse literacy needs. In this process, we also have to understand that being a culturally responsive teacher is more than simply teaching lessons. It is a way of thinking that encompasses being intentional about inclusive and equitable practices, embracing the richness of students' lives and communities, celebrating the funds of knowledge our students bring to the classroom (Moll, Amanti, Neff, & Gonzalez, 1992), and disrupting the status quo. It is also imperative that in this process, we consider how we can be reflective teachers and understand that being a culturally responsive teacher is an ongoing process. For example, we have to continually ask ourselves questions about our biases and beliefs about the students we teach.

STOP AND REFLECT

- What do I believe about teaching?
- What do I believe about children?
- How do these beliefs influence my teaching practices?

We approach this book from our experiences teaching children in grades K–12, providing professional development to educators, and our perspectives as literacy teacher educators. We have two goals in this book. First, we want to provide support for and examples of culturally responsive lessons and activities we have implemented in our own teaching in K–12 and university classrooms to provide tangible examples for readers to use in their own classrooms. We want to support teachers and teacher educators who are already aware of the abundance of research showing that when instruction is presented to students in ways that help them connect to their own cultures and experiences, they will find success in the classroom (Emdin, 2016; Gay, 2010; Ladson-Billings, 1995; Villegas & Lucas, 2007) and to extend the conversation from *why* culturally responsive teaching is important to examples of *how* to implement culturally responsive literacy instruction.

Second, we want to provide support for and examples of preparing teachers to recognize K–12 classroom literacy practices that are often well intentioned but inequitable to children. The work we do does not exist in isolation; educating teachers involves more than the teacher education program. The teacher education program must complement and compete with the influences of PSTs' preconceived beliefs and the school and district in which they are placed for field experiences (observations and practice), thus making it difficult to identify the impact of the curriculum alone (Zoss, Holbrook, McGrail, & Albers, 2014). Although teacher education curricula have been criticized for failing to link theory and practice, creating spaces to observe, engage in, critique, and discuss praxis may help bridge that gap. This contextualization is particularly essential when preparing PSTs to work with children from economically disadvantaged and/or ethnically and racially diverse backgrounds (Laman, Miller, & López-Robertson, 2012); if the experiences provided do not allow for facilitated discussion and include instruction around culture and cultural practices, field experiences in diverse communities may only reinforce negative stereotypes (Ladson-Billings, 2000).

From our lens as teacher educators, we share how we actively teach our PSTs to recognize culturally irrelevant literacy instruction (Souto-Manning et al., 2018) in the field with the intent of opening spaces for more inclusive literacy instructional practices in their visions and actions as (future) teachers. From our positions as teacher educators, we have the ability to interrupt and disrupt literacy teaching that ignores K–12 students' cultures and lived experiences by modeling culturally responsive literacy instruction in our classrooms. Through our modeling, we can call attention to literacy practices that may be well meant but are irrelevant to or neglectful of the realities of their students' lives, and we demonstrate how to recognize and change these practices in their own instruction. We hope that by sharing these examples from our own teaching and research, teacher educators and practicing teachers will find this book helpful when considering ways to disrupt practices already in place and add new cultural responsiveness into their teaching, translating into more equitable literacy practices in K–12 classrooms.

We understand that K–12 teachers can see culturally responsive instruction as one more thing to do or add to their instructional plans (Souto-Manning et al., 2018), or they may be concerned that they will face resistance from their administration and/or student families. We counteract these concerns and frame this work in everyday teaching by acknowledging the connections to literacy curriculum standards (Overstreet, 2018; Ryan & Hermann-Wilmarth, 2018) in each chapter. Although curriculum standards were not written for diverse students, we disrupt literacy standards by emphasizing the connection between research-based literacy practices, standards, and culturally responsive instruction to show that this approach is not "one more thing." As Mikkaka has written previously,

There are opportunities within the Standards for teachers to make important curricular decisions and to do what is best for the children in their particular classrooms. The Standards don't mandate a particular curriculum or approach, nor do they limit topics of study to only what is within their pages. Despite misinterpretation and misuse by various entities, the intent of the Standards is to allow teachers the freedom "to provide students with whatever tools and knowledge their professional judgment and experience identify as most helpful for meeting the goals set out in the Standards." It is up to the teachers to move beyond what has been privileged by being explicitly written in the CCSS. (Overstreet, 2018, p. 223)

Culturally responsive instruction is an integral part of the learning process, and it provides evidence to families and administrators that we *can* and *should* simultaneously meet the diverse needs of our students while providing high-quality literacy instruction that addresses the curriculum standards.

DEFINING CULTURALLY RESPONSIVE

When we consider how we enact culturally responsive instruction, we must start by defining what we mean by using the phrase. Each of us came to our individual sense of how to be a culturally responsive teacher who approaches instruction from a critical and socially just perspective. This means that we approach teaching using a social justice lens, which is "a philosophy, an approach, and *actions* that embody treating all people with fairness, respect, dignity, and generosity" (Nieto & Bode, 2012, p. 12) to consider how we can better affirm and respond to our students' cultures and lived experiences to create inclusive and equitable classrooms. From this lens, we see teaching as an opportunity to teach *for* social justice. By becoming aware of and learning ways to disrupt inequities in K–12 literacy instruction, teachers can work toward more equitable instruction.

When we consider the terms we use in this book about our own teaching and research, we want to be clear that we acknowledge and appreciate terms that have been used to describe culturally responsive instruction. We are grateful to the scholars before us who introduced terms such as "culturally relevant," "culturally responsive," "culturally sustaining," "social justice," and so on (Gay, 2018; Ladson-Billings, 1995; Paris & Alim, 2017) to describe a stance and an approach to teaching with equity at the forefront of our minds. Similar to how Geneva Gay (2018) points out that a variety of terms exist that educators and researchers use to describe this framework, we will use "culturally responsive" in this book because, like Gay, we "feel it represents a compilation of ideas and explanations from a variety of scholars" (p. 36). We use the term "culturally responsive" because, as Gay (2010) asserts,

> Culturally responsive teaching can be defined as using the cultural knowledge, prior experiences, frames of reference, and performance styles of ethnically diverse students to make learning encounters more relevant to and effective for them. It teaches to and through the strengths of these students. (p. 31)

Although Gay focuses explicitly on race, culture, and ethnicity, she invites scholars to define diversity for themselves. Gay (2013) states that others "may focus instead on gender, sexual orientation, social class, or linguistic diversity as specific contexts for actualizing general principles of culturally responsive teaching" as long as they "make their commitments explicit and how they exemplify the general principles and values of teaching to and through cultural diversity" (pp. 52–53).

We use the term "culturally responsive" because we want to advocate affirming students' cultures in a way that values the experiences and communities of the individuals within our classrooms. Although we recognize the multitude of diverse identities in our classrooms and in the classrooms across the nation, in this book, we focus on diversity that includes race and ethnicity as well as gender identity, sexual orientation, and religion. Affirming students' cultures and experiences is central in our work as culturally responsive teachers, and we deliberately use this term in our modeling and conversations with our PSTs and in our work with K–12 educators.

We are drawn to and advocate for literacy instruction as a conduit to equity and socially just teaching for several reasons. One overall motivating factor is that language is used as a way to instill cultural norms, which assumes power or authority over the way things should be, within everyday practices. For example, teachers often use the terms "struggling," "at risk," or "behind" to describe a child's literacy knowledge or development. Each of these terms positions the child as lacking in comparison to a mythical standard or norm and conveys a deficit perspective of the child's literacy knowledge and development. But how can a five-year-old child be behind in their literacy development or knowledge? Instead, we advocate that literacy instruction builds on and accesses the richness of students' lives and communities to affirm the funds of knowledge our students bring into the classroom.

Returning to the five-year-old child who is labeled as "behind," using a culturally responsive perspective, we can see that the child has had rich literacy experiences in their community and home. However, the literacy experiences may not align with traditional teaching practices reflecting middle-class, European American cultural values; therefore, we recognize that deficit-based notions of diverse students continue to permeate traditional school thinking and practices. Thus, we advocate critiquing and incrementally moving away from such practices to instruction that recognizes the explicit connection between culture and learning and that sees students' cultural capital as an asset and not a detriment to their school success. In this way, we avoid positioning learners as flawed and position them instead as individuals with a wealth of knowledge that they can continue to develop.

As literacy educators, we are intentional about inclusive literacy practices and advocate for teachers to work against inequities by disrupting power relationships that legitimize language. We are also intentional about how we and society understand our experiences through powerful and authoritative language. Additionally, language provides a lens into how we understand ourselves and how we share our identities with others. As teachers, we have a great responsibility to our students (of all ages) to recognize and affirm their identities in our classrooms and in our teaching decisions (Ahmed, 2018a; Souto-Manning et al., 2018). We also have responsibilities to our students to recognize how our own identities impact our biases about socially constructed categories, our understandings of these categories, and, ultimately, our teaching practices that perpetuate our biases (Ahmed, 2018a; Howard, Overstreet, & Ticknor, 2018; Howard & Ticknor, 2019; Souto-Manning et al., 2018; Ticknor, Overstreet, & Howard, 2020).

Each of us approach culturally responsive teaching from similar theoretical lenses yet different perspectives due to our identities, cultures, and experiences. Because who we are impacts how we view our students and how we teach, our lived experiences impact us in unique ways. Through our work together as teacher educators and researchers, we have commonalities about how we approach teaching from a socially just and equity stance. Although our schooling and teaching experiences vary widely, we each entered the teaching profession in our early twenties, and our experiences of culture and community extended into how we wanted to be teachers in our individual classrooms. We deeply considered how we could recognize and affirm our students' cultures and lived experiences that were often different than our own, and actively learned how to be more culturally responsive in our approach to teaching and the importance of infusing culturally responsive practices into our classrooms in support of PSTs (Dyches & Boyd, 2017; Howard, Overstreet, & Ticknor, 2018; Jimenez, 2014).

THE IMPORTANCE OF IDENTITY WORK

Mikkaka emphasizes throughout each course she teaches, "Who you are impacts how you teach. Who they are impacts how they learn." We do not come to our classrooms, take off our outside selves, and become some sort of robot creatures, devoid of feelings, experiences, unconscious bias, and societal influences. Nor do our students leave their out-of-school selves at the door, no matter how much traditional schooling structures attempt to force them to do so. As educators, we have to know ourselves and how the multitude of experiences, beliefs, and influences of our lives shape our practice. Parr and Campbell (2011) discuss how many of our personal stories and experiences may be shaped by traditional, middle-class experiences; therefore, we must deconstruct and problematize these experiences and stories that shape our identities. Similarly, McCarthey and Moje (2002) encourage us to challenge our own identities as we both acknowledge and *challenge* our "sense of self." Exploring who we are and how that connects to how we teach and engage with literacy is essential to how we prepare to engage in culturally responsive teaching. If we choose not to attend to our identities and the identities of our students, we are not choosing neutrality; we are implicit in perpetuating un-just systems when we refuse to acknowledge them.

Muhammad (2020) defines identity as "composed of notions of who we are, who others say we are (in both positive and negative ways), and whom we desire to be" (p. 67). As educators, we may think that our identities and our biases do not influence how and what we teach, but let us explore for a moment how they do. We believe that our identities are shaped by our experiences, our individual sense of self, and the ownership we take on of others' perceptions of us. We also believe that identity shapes how we view and understand the world. Why is this important in literacy instruction? What role do our identities play in educational spaces? Understanding how our identities differ from others can help us disrupt the single narratives we have been taught and the single narratives we teach based on our identities. To begin this work, we have to first explore, interpret, and interrogate our own identities so we can ask ourselves how our identities can help us push against the systems of oppression.

For Anne, her early experiences of school included mostly white spaces, monolingual interactions, and traditional gender roles. Anne learned from an early age that fitting into these spaces benefited her as a student. She found that much of how she learned to view the world mirrored much of the K–12 curriculum, her classmates' experiences and cultures, as well as her teachers' cultures. Additionally, her father's ancestral Norwegian heritage and family's agricultural knowledge taught her from an early age that recognizing and af-firming cultural experiences was important to her identity and self-conception both inside and outside of school.

Although Anne's hometown offered her few chances to learn firsthand about diverse cultures and communities, she sought books, people, and spaces—when available to her—to learn about and interact with different cultures or experiences. However, it was not until college when Anne first encountered teachers of color and a curriculum that provided windows into cultures and communities different than her own. College gave Anne multiple opportunities to learn about the richness of diverse communities and cultures, which translated into how she envisioned herself as an elementary teacher and the communities where she wanted to teach. Anne knew that learner identities and validated life experiences were important to meaningful learning, and she wanted to teach in communities where her identities and experiences were not the majority.

Anne student taught on Navajo Nation and then became a fourth-grade teacher in North Las Vegas, Nevada. At first, Anne's identities as a white, monolingual woman from a small blue-collar Midwest town did not translate into her vision of being a culturally responsive teacher in these spaces. In fact, they did not translate at all. Anne engaged in deep self-reflection and critical questioning of her own identities and beliefs about instruction. She wondered if she could be a teacher in these spaces and sought mentors who could support her in learning how to be more knowledgeable about her students' communities and cultures as well as resources to make more culturally responsive teaching decisions.

Anne also learned how to be an advocate for and an ally to her elementary-aged students and their families who identified as LGBTQ. Although Anne had several experiences with adult friends who identified as LGBTQ, Anne was unprepared to support her LGBTQ students and their families. She sought resources and built her knowledge about her students' identities and experiences so that she was better prepared. Again, Anne's perseverance and passion for affirming her students' cultures and communities in classroom learning to make it more meaningful and more relevant drove her to learn how to be more culturally responsive in her teaching decisions and disrupt misconceptions, biases, and stereotypes she held about identities unlike her own.

Christy's experiences growing up in school were very different from the students she taught. For example, she grew up in predominantly white schools throughout her K–12 schooling and often found herself as the only Black student in the classroom. In this position, she often felt that her identity was erased and her experiences were not valued. Not only did she not see herself in her peers, teachers, or administrators, but she also failed to see herself in the literature she was required to read. At school, she felt very little connection to her own culture, and in school settings, she felt the need to assimilate to the whiteness, neglecting and even hiding her own rich cultural experiences for fear of feeling even more isolated. High school was the first time she encountered a text by a person of color in school; it was Maya Angelou's (1984) *I Know Why the Caged Bird Sings*. In reading this required text and seeing experiences with people who looked like her being valued, Christy's perspectives of school began to change. Her English teacher celebrated the works of Maya Angelou, her culture, and her experiences. For Christy, this was the first time she had seen Black culture and experience celebrated in school outside of the realm of Martin Luther King and Rosa Parks.

Years later when Christy became a classroom teacher, she was hired in a school with a very different cultural makeup than the schools she attended. Christy taught only one white student her first year of teaching, and the rest of her students were students of color. Christy's white principal assumed that because Christy was a teacher of color, she would be the perfect fit for her students. Here, Christy wrestled again with her identity as a Black, middle-class woman with experiences only in predominantly white schools. She was now expected to be an amazing teacher for students of color when she had never been afforded the opportunity to engage in the learning process *as* a student of color with her experiences acknowledged and valued in schools. Anything she learned about her culture had been taught at home and at church. Therefore, she began by teaching the way she had experienced teaching and the way she had been taught to teach, with a focus on skills, testing, and white-dominated literature.

This teaching was contrary to who Christy was and who she wanted to be as an educator. It was also contrary to the needs of her students. As Christy began to acknowledge the role of her experiences, beliefs about teaching, and her identity, she realized that school had not and was not a place of embracing cultural knowledge and experiences. She wanted to provide experiences for her students that she so desperately wanted in school. However, because she had never experienced this, she was unsure of how to do so. After self-reflection and focusing on building a classroom community, with the help of her students, Christy learned how to value her own identity as well as the identity of her students, helping them feel visible in ways she had never been afforded in her classroom experiences. She realized the importance of advocating for students and creating spaces to foster and celebrate cultural connections, using students' rich funds of knowledge as a resource in designing authentic classroom experiences.

For Mikkaka, school was a safe haven. Growing up as the only child of a young, single mom who worked a lot and tended to indulge in her own pleasures during her free time, Mikkaka often spent time alone reading and writing. Her teachers valued her studious nature, her intelligence, and her quiet obedience, while Mikkaka eagerly soaked up their validation. Although she attended fairly diverse schools, her teachers were mostly white, and, like

Christy, Mikkaka rarely saw herself reflected in the curricula that her white teachers followed. Mikkaka's passion for reading led her to stumble on mirror texts from time to time, and when she found a book she liked, she usually read it until it was worn thin. Books like *Phillip Hall Likes Me, I Reckon Maybe* by Bette Green (1974), *Roll of Thunder, Hear My Cry* by Mildred D. Taylor (1976), and *M. C. Higgins the Great* by Virginia Hamilton (1974) were dog-eared and tattered with love.

Still, Mikkaka consumed mostly white culture and was teased for "talking white." She remembers the pain of a Black gym teacher in fourth grade saying, in front of a small group of Black girls whom the teacher favored, that Mikkaka was "brainwashed" by the white teachers she loved so much. That was the beginning of Mikkaka feeling out of place in both Black and white spaces. At home, she lived in overcrowded apartment complexes where she read books instead of playing with the other children. When she was younger, she had jumped rope and hula-hooped with her peers, but her bookishness and comments like the one from the gym teacher had eventually separated her from them. In secondary school, Mikkaka remained ambivalent about her identity but was encouraged continuously by her teachers to strive for college and all of her goals. She often read and wrote about race, still trying to figure out where she belonged. By the time she graduated college, she had left behind that confused girl who didn't feel Black enough. She had minored in pan-African studies and found Black role models. She was determined to teach at a school where she could support poor, Black children like her.

Instead, she was offered a coveted position at an affluent and predominantly white elementary school. The parents at this school wore designer clothes and high heels and brought sushi lunches for their children. Most of the teachers were similarly well-off and older, with spouses and children. Mikkaka felt starkly different as one of the few Black teachers and someone who had never lived in a home that wasn't rented. She was a closeted bisexual, ambivalent about marriage and gender norms, and pretty sure she never wanted children. She worried that by taking this job, she had betrayed the children like her. However, it proved to be exactly the place for her. She soon realized how much the privileged children of all races at her school needed to see and learn from someone like her. The children who were bused miles across town from the projects needed her as well. The little girls, both Black and white, who loved to play with the white girls' long straight hair grew excited about her large Afro. The Black boys who got into big trouble for minor infractions based on cultural differences benefited from her perspective and advocacy. Mikkaka knew that her work and her identity were important, and she knew without a doubt that she would be an educator forever.

One common thread that we used in our quest to be more culturally responsive teachers was literacy. As classroom teachers, we quickly found that if we asked our K–12 students to talk, listen, read, write, and draw, we learned about their lives from them, and we could connect school learning to their lived experiences. Much in the same way we learned how to incorporate our K–12 students' lives into our classrooms, we now provide similar opportunities for our teacher education students in our literacy education courses to view literacy as a conduit to meaning making.

We encourage readers to consider the role of their identities in their classrooms, their instruction, and their beliefs about students to make their classrooms culturally responsive spaces. There are many resources teachers can use to explore their identities, there is no one strategy to use, and there are several activities that teachers can engage in to help in this process. One example of how Christy has engaged PSTs in exploring their identities is to spend several days at the beginning of the semester asking PSTs to reflect on who they are and the experiences they bring to the classrooms. She tells them that this is important to consider before we facilitate conversations with students, and we can't do this without unpacking our identities. For example, PSTs can respond to the following example questions (some specific to literacy and some more general questions) through journal writing, poetry, or creating visual images or another medium:

- What literacy experiences have shaped who you are as a reader today?
- What/who has influenced your thinking about the world (education, religion, current events, and so on)?
- How does your identity influence how you respond to the media (music, news stories, television shows)?
- How does who you are influence how you discuss texts/characters with students?
- What cultural experiences do you bring with you to the classroom? How does this influence your instructional decisions?
- What theories do you bring with you to the classroom? How does this influence your instructional decisions?
- What ideals do you bring with you to the classroom? How does this influence your instructional decisions?
- How do your memories, experiences, and knowledge help you make sense of texts? How might this sense making be different for people with different identities?
- What issues are important to you? How do you think your identity contributes to the importance of these issues?

Once teachers have engaged in their own identity work, they can begin engaging in identity work with K–12 students in ways that affirm students' identities. Some engaging activities for helping students affirm their identities can be found in Sara Ahmed's (2018b) book *Being the Change: Lessons and Strategies to Teach Social Comprehension*. Examples of these activities include creating identity webs, exploring the histories of names, and creating "Where I'm From" poems. Validating and affirming our students' identities means making space for students to share and be who they are. In her book *Cultivating Genius: An Equity Framework for Culturally and Historically Responsive Literacy*, Muhammad (2020) warns, "If they don't know themselves, others will tell them who they are, in ways that may not be positive or accurate" (p. 70). Muhammad also provides resources and strategies for students to explore their identities, including a "Who Are You" exercise, creating digital stories, and studying the histories of communities. Engaging in identity work with students gives them an opportunity to unpack the brilliance and beauty of who they are and to bring their full selves into our classroom spaces.

Another example of how Christy engages teachers in interrogating their identities and biases is through sharing books that do not represent the dominant narrative, such as *The Proudest Blue: A Story of Hijab and Family* (Muhammad, 2019), a book about a Muslim American girl that describes her experiences as her sister begins wearing her hijab to school. This is a beautifully written and illustrated book, with a moving, powerful author's message at the end. The words and images will take your breath away, and at the conclusion of the story, PSTs always discuss the beautiful images and language. However, at least one PST will voice a concern about sharing this book in the classroom because it's about (whisper) religion and parents and caregivers may not approve. In response to this question, it's important to consider the question of identity. To begin, which parents will not approve? The Muslim American parents? The Black parents? The Christian parents? As we think of these questions, why is it fair to value the response of one group of parents over another group? Do we read stories about Christmas in elementary school? Do we teach "The Gift of the Magi" (Henry, 1906) in middle and high schools? Don't our teaching standards even include the Bible as the single example of a "religious text" that students should consider when looking at themes in fictional texts? How is this different? In these discussions, Christy asks teachers to consider what it is about your identity and experiences that makes you concerned about teaching these texts, then to explore the biases they hold that make them see teaching about diversity as a debate and what biases make them question the validity of these books and experiences and/or beliefs in classroom spaces. Finally, Christy asks them what parts of their identities contribute to these concerns.

Once we begin the ongoing work of interrogating our own identities, we can help those we teach to explore their own identities and consider who they bring to the works they read and the news stories they see. In this way, we create spaces in our curriculum that respond to students' identities and validate who they bring to this work from a strengths-based perspective that is celebrated, not oppressed, and that can avoid harmful instruction. We have seen teachers ask their students to write from the perspective of a slave or to argue for the justification of slavery as part of an "argument-writing" unit. These types of activities are curriculum violence (Jones, 2020), as they minimize the experiences of oppressed people, they debate the humanity of people, and they give the idea that oppressed identities are easily put on and taken off.

SITUATING OUR CURRENT WORK

Currently, we teach at a large public university in the southern United States, and the courses we teach include undergraduate and graduate literacy education courses for preservice and in-service teachers. Our university offers many pathways to state licensure, which means that our students vary in age, experiences, and identities. Overwhelmingly, though, our undergraduate PSTs identify as white and female. According to the National Center for Education Statistics (2016), 84 percent of U.S. public school teachers identify as white, and 85 percent identify as female, mirroring the demographics of the PSTs in our classes.

Similar to Anne's experiences as a K–12 student, many of our PSTs have not had teachers of color or classmates with different experiences from their own. Anecdotally, our PSTs report that they want to be effective teachers who value and honor their students' lives and identities. However, they also share that they do not know how to enact this in their instruction. Similar to the responses in the opening scene from Christy's class, this is due to their lack of experience that inequities in education exist or instructional practices do not benefit or recognize all students' ways of knowing or funds of knowledge. These views may be due to different life and cultural experiences without an opportunity for examination before our classes.

Other PSTs tell us that although they care about kids, they imagine they will need to teach using the same methods and materials as their same grade-level or content colleagues or use the programs already in place at their school. And still other PSTs tell us they are fearful that parents or colleagues will disagree with selecting materials or methods that affirm cultures or experiences that have been historically silenced. Finally, some of our PSTs are unaware that inequities exist in society and report that our culturally responsive teaching challenges their beliefs. We try to disrupt their preconceptions—and often inaccurate information—about students from communities and cultures different from their own by engaging them in discussions about diversity and culturally responsive instruction.

As we have shared before (Howard et al., 2018), talking and reading about the need for culturally responsive instruction is not enough. Our PSTs need to see and hear how we make culturally responsive teaching decisions, and they need to engage in these teaching practices as students and as teachers who will then implement similar activities with their own K–12 students. This means that we model our questions and concerns related to teaching from a culturally responsive stance, and we position self-reflection and questioning as part of the process of teaching from a stance of equity and social justice. We are explicit about why and how we make our teaching decisions, such as selecting materials that are responsive and inclusive of students' cultures (see chapter 2), so that our PSTs can see our thinking. We are also deliberate in how we model lessons they may teach in their classrooms so that they not only experience what culturally responsive teaching looks and feels like as a student but also can ask questions of us and share their experiences of the activities with us and each other. We intend for this type of discussion to model and initiate the kind of teacher self-reflection and questioning that is critical to culturally responsive instruction in the safety of our university classrooms.

Collectively, we have more than 50 years of experience as educators, have provided professional development in a broad range of U.S. geographic regions, and have worked with a variety of educators. We base our work with PSTs within the context of the range of K–12 teachers we know exist in our present region and in our previous work in different regions of the United States. We bring our experiences as classroom teachers, as literacy educators and researchers, and as community members to model, think aloud, and discuss culturally responsive instructional decisions we hope will impact a new generation of K–12 teachers. By supporting teacher educators, practicing teachers, and PSTs in doing the hard work of challenging and changing unjust teaching practices, we ultimately hope to deliberately disrupt inequitable literacy instruction for K–12 students.

We have also built a network of educators to reflect together about our practice. In the uncertainty that sometimes surrounds this work, we have come to the realization that we cannot do this work alone. Instead, we ask questions of ourselves and each other; we seek advice and guidance for our work with teacher education students as we strive to become better culturally responsive teachers. Informally, we talk about teaching with our colleagues, and we seek resources—both scholarly and practitioner based—to support how we teach. Through these networks, we are working together to continue to be more reflective in our practices.

Formally, we have created a teaching and research team where we meet to discuss our teaching, our identities, our perceptions, and how our teaching is impacted by who we are and how we conceptualize teaching for social justice. We also conduct self-studies where we observe our own and each other's teaching, examine our students' responses to our teaching, and develop new approaches to teaching that culturally affirm our students and their (future) students' cultures. Recently, we have begun to study how our PSTs, in particular our undergraduate students enrolled in an initial teacher education program, respond to our teaching. The example lessons we share in this book are part of this study.

OVERVIEW OF THIS BOOK

As you read this book, we will ask you to keep in mind several big ideas. These guiding principles are crucial to this work. We will frequently remind you of these guiding principles throughout the chapters, with details on how the principles apply to particular reflections or lessons. Often, this will take the form of an offset text box beginning with the word "remember."

Guiding Principles

- *Culturally responsive instruction is not one-size-fits-all.* By definition, this type of instruction is contingent on context. You cannot and should not pick up the lesson examples in this book and deliver them directly to your students. You must make considerations for the unique contexts in which you teach and learn and instead take up the principles guiding this work.
- *Culturally responsive instruction is not activities.* One cannot simply do our suggested activities and consider their instruction to be culturally responsive. You must also "do the work." This means changing your ways of thinking about teaching and students, engaging in deep reflection and committing to a lifelong learning process of staying current on appropriate and affirming language choices, issues of equity, and societal trends.
- *Culturally responsive instruction is not just for "those" kids.* This is for everyone. All of our students deserve to be properly prepared to live in a diverse world. Affirming their cultures does not mean that you teach this way only if you have "diverse" kids in your classroom. For starters, diver-

sity is far more than what you can see, so you must expand your thinking. Further, this work requires a disruption of traditional teaching, which is rooted in white, cisgender, Christian, abled, heteronormative, middle-class ideals. This has to be done in *all* classrooms so that *all* children can see themselves *and* others as a valid and valued part of the curriculum.

• *Culturally responsive instruction is not "one more thing."* This isn't an add-on or one more entry on teachers' already long to-do lists. Culturally responsive teaching is a method, a lens, a frame through which all of your teaching passes. You don't set aside a block of time for culturally responsive teaching; you do it all day: math, literacy, science, social studies, art, physical education, music, and all other subjects can and should be taught in culturally responsive ways and with a culturally responsive intentional way of thinking.

With this in mind, we hope that readers understand that culturally responsive instruction is not about boxed or prescribed lessons. Culturally responsive instruction is about knowing the students in front of you and the ways in which you can affirm students' identities and experiences as you develop the curriculum.

ORGANIZATION OF THIS BOOK

This book is organized into chapters around topics central to literacy instruction: material selection, instructional language, and reading response. Each chapter opens with fictional vignettes of literacy instruction in K–12 classrooms. We offer a vignette from an elementary and from a secondary setting in each chapter. The vignettes provide examples as a way to situate how teachers may be using research-based literacy practices while ignoring the identities and experiences of their students.

Next, we share theories and concepts that are often related to culturally responsive teaching specific to literacy instruction we seek to disrupt in each vignette. We use these theories and concepts to make visible how the literacy practices in the vignettes could be reimagined to integrate more culturally responsive strategies. In this discussion, we highlight how we prepare our PSTs to recognize common yet culturally irrelevant K–12 classroom literacy practices in the field. Our intent is that readers will see examples of how they may make more visible similar practices in their specific teaching contexts.

Once we have disrupted the vignettes, we apply the chapter theories and concepts in lesson examples that we have implemented in our literacy education courses with our PSTs. Each lesson includes intended grade levels, standards, and curriculum resources. We also include how we reflect on and encourage PSTs to think about our teaching decisions related to culturally responsive teaching, including connecting learning through a culturally responsive lens to standards. We want readers to see how a culturally responsive lens is embedded in decisions teachers make about instruction. We hope readers see these example lessons as resources and models of how to include more culturally responsive and affirming strategies in their literacy instruction. We do not intend for readers to use our lessons as templates to follow because culturally responsive teaching is not one-size-fits-all for teachers or students.

Throughout each chapter, we offer reminders about the principles guiding culturally responsive literacy instruction listed in the guiding principles. We want readers to continually reflect on these principles and see their connections to theories, concepts, and practice in each chapter. Finally, each chapter ends with reflection questions based on chapter information to prompt readers to consider their own practices and consider ways to be more culturally responsive teachers for their students and in their local communities.

STOP AND REFLECT

- What is your guiding principle, your north star, the belief that guides you as an educator?
- How diverse were the neighborhoods I grew up in and the schools I attended?
- What types of interactions did I have with individuals from backgrounds different from my own?
- Who were the primary persons who helped shape my perspectives of individuals from different groups? How were their opinions formed?
- Have I ever harbored prejudiced thoughts toward people from different backgrounds? If I do harbor prejudiced thoughts, what effects do such thoughts have on students who come from those backgrounds?
- How is that reflected in the instructional decisions I will make, the environment I will create in my classroom, and how I will interact with students and families?

Chapter One

Material Selection
for Literacy Instruction

Scenario 1

Mr. Allen teaches kindergarten. His students are ethnically, racially, and linguistically diverse. They include Black, white, and Latinx, as well as Pakistani, Filipino, Haitian, Sudanese, and combinations thereof. His class includes children whose parents hail from eight different countries, speak multiple languages at home, and are at varying stages of English mastery. Of his students who have been in the United States for generations, many grew up within a three-mile radius of the school and have never left the city.

Mr. Allen knows that phonological awareness is a key early literacy skill, so he spends time working with sounds during whole- and small-group instruction. He uses lots of pictures so that his emergent readers can understand without having mastered letter–sound correspondence. He found lots of picture sets on the internet. At the word work center, Ahmed, Semaj, Angie, Nicole, and Emmanuel are sorting words into the families "-at" and "-an" using the pictures shown in figure 1.1.

Figure 1.1.   Picture Cards. *https://www.pexels.com*

Scenario 2

Mrs. Travis is preparing novel units for her sixth graders. She wants to allow them choice so that they'll get excited about reading. Her class is predominantly white and middle class, so she's sure that lots of books will appeal to them as long as she has a good mix of "boy books" and "girl books." She selects six high-interest books of varying difficulty so that all of her readers can pick a "just right" text. Her final list includes the texts shown in table 2.1.

Mrs. Travis wants to make sure her students are reading the text, so she found questions for each book on the internet. The questions ask surface-level, detailed questions so she knows she will be able to determine if they have read the text. Each night, she assigns the students pages to read and multiple-choice questions to answer. When the students come to class each day, Mrs. Travis gives the students 10 minutes to meet in their groups. During this time, the group leader is given the answer key to the questions, and the students review their answers. At the end of the 10 minutes, Mrs. Travis assigns new page numbers and questions for homework.

Most literacy educators have heard of Bishop's (1990) metaphor of books as mirrors and windows; children should have access to books in which they see themselves reflected (mirrors) *and* books that allow them to see into the lives of others (windows). Students should have access to books that feature characters representing a broad range of races, ethnicities, languages, gender identities, sexual orientations, and abilities. The Cooperative Children's Book Center (CCBC) at the University of Wisconsin, Madison, collects and shares data on racial representation in children's literature each year. Sarah Park Dahlen, an associate professor in the Master of Library and Information Science Program at St. Catherine University in St. Paul, Minnesota, and illustrator David Huyck (2019) use CCBC data to create a popular infographic (see figure 2.2) that demonstrates how, racially, some children aren't getting adequate mirrors and windows. White children are far more likely to have rich, varied, and accurate mirrors while getting few, often distorted windows. Fueling that distortion is the fact that the books written *about* people of color are often written *by* white authors. As a matter of fact, many books about diverse populations (e.g., people with disabilities) are written by authors who do not share the identities of the people they're writing about. While this is not to suggest that authors cannot write outside of their identities, it is important to recognize the richness added to diverse literature when diverse authors are given opportunities to tell their own stories. Staying current and locating books written by #ownvoices authors (Corinne Duyvis, https://www.corinneduyvis.net/ownvoices) can be a challenge if educators do not know where to look. Two educators who can help are Laura Jimenez, who writes about books with LGBTQ characters and themes (https://booktoss.org), and Debbie Reese, who focuses on American Indians in literature (https://

Table 1.1. Mrs. Travis's Text Set

Text	Cover Description	Character Information
The Lion, the Witch, and the Wardrobe by C. S. Lewis	The most recent version of the cover is a close-up image of a lion. Previous editions have included several children with the lion; all present as white.	As this book is a Christian allegory, it has stark religious overtones throughout. While the characters' races are not explicitly discussed and there are fantasy elements that include sentient and talking animals and mythical creatures, the story centers on a family of white children. The 2005 movie adaptation cast consisted almost entirely of white actors. The characters are restricted to traditional gender roles, and any overt sexuality reads as heterosexual.
The Lightning Thief by Rick Riordan	On the cover of the edition illustrated by John Rocco, a boy (roughly middle school aged and white), stands in rough water while holding a sword. The boy stands across from Medusa, several skeletons, a minotaur, a lion, a snake, and something with wings that is partially obscured by the title, all of whom seem to be poised to attack the child. In the background, there is a city with lightning above it. Other editions show the back of a white child, standing in rough water (one while on the head of a large statue of Poseidon) and holding a sword and a horn of some sort looking up at a city with lightning strikes above it.	This book is based heavily on Greek mythology and references a number of gods and demigods. The main character has attention-deficit/hyperactivity disorder and dyslexia, and there is an LGBTQ representation with some of the characters. There was a 2010 movie adaptation that has been criticized for not being true to the books.
Hatchet by Gary Paulsen	On one edition of the cover, there is an animated headshot of a young white boy, partially overlaid with the silhouette of a hatchet, a wolf howling at a moon, and an airplane. In the background is a simple landscape with mountains and a forest. Another version of the cover is a silhouette of a hatchet in the center, with an abstract forest in the background, along with a wolf silhouette.	The story focuses on a 13-year-old white boy and the way in which he is handling his apparently heterosexual parents' recent divorce. There is no mention of the character's race, which unfortunately is indicative of America's tendency to only include labels when someone does not fit the "norm" of white, cis, able-bodied, etc. There are very few characters in the book, and aside from the pilot, all are in the main character's family.

(continued)

Table 1.1. *(continued)*

Text	Cover Description	Character Information
The Wishing Spell by Chris Colfer	The cover features two white, blond-haired children falling. In the background is a castle, a tower, a beanstalk, and a gingerbread house. Surrounding the main picture is a drawing of presumably Snow White near a cauldron with apples, Sleeping Beauty near a spinning wheel, a frog wearing a tie and jacket while carrying a jar and a stack of books, two fairies holding a glass shoe, and a large black rat or wolf with red eyes and an open mouthing showing its teeth.	The main characters, a set of blond-haired, blue-eyed twins, are lost in a fairy-tale world in which the other characters are white, animals, or mythical creatures. Any relationships within the story appear heterosexual.
The Bad Beginning; Or, Orphans! by Lemony Snicket	This cover features three white children standing in front of the remains of a burned-down house. In another edition of the cover, three white children are standing in a doorway with an older man looking down at them. There is a stark contrast between the colorful city in the background and the bluish-gray of the man and the interior of the doorway.	Within the book, the characters, where described, are white. There has been a movie in 2004 and a television series from 2017 to 2019 based on this book and the rest of the series. Within the television series, there is a broader range of diversity within the cast with regard to both race and sexuality.
Tuck Everlasting by Natalie Babbitt	There have been several different covers. One featured a white girl wearing a dress and holding a frog. Another cover shows a small house by a lake where there is a silhouette of two people in a small boat and the reflection of the house.	The main character is a young white girl who lives with her mother and grandmother. She is considering a heterosexual relationship with one of the Tucks. Two movie adaptations were made in 1981 and 2002, both of which had predominantly white casts.

americanindiansinchildrensliterature.blogspot.com). Both of these educators and scholars offer recommendations, critiques, and resources for locating literature that affirms and accurately represents identities in literature written for K–12 students.

DIVERSITY IN CHILDREN'S BOOKS 2018

Percentage of books depicting characters from diverse backgrounds based on the 2018 publishing statistics compiled by the Cooperative Children's Book Center, School of Education, University of Wisconsin-Madison:
ccbc.education.wisc.edu/books/pcstats.asp

| 1% | 5% | 7% | 10% | 27% | 50% |
| American Indians/ First Nations | Latinx | Asian Pacific Islander/Asian Pacific American | African/ African American | Animals/Other | White |

The CCBC Inventory includes 3,134 books published in 2018. This graphic would not have been possible without the statistics compiled by the CCBC, and the review and feedback we received from Edith Campbell, Molly Beth Griffin, K. T. Horning, Debbie Reese, Ebony Elizabeth Thomas, and Madeline Tyner. Many thanks.

Illustration by David Huyck, in consultation with Sarah Park Dahlen.
Released under a Creative Commons BY-SA license: https://creativecommons.org/licenses/by-sa/4.0/

Figure 1.2. CCBC Diversity in Children's Books. Huyck, David, and Sarah Park Dahlen (2019, June 19). *Diversity in Children's Books 2018. sarahpark.com blog. Created in consultation with Edith Campbell, Molly Beth Griffin, K. T. Horning, Debbie Reese, Ebony Elizabeth Thomas, and Madeline Tyner, with statistics compiled by the Cooperative Children's Book Center, School of Education, University of Wisconsin, Madison: https:// ccbc.education.wisc.edu/literature-resources/ccbc-diversity-statistics/books-by-about-poc-fnn. Retrieved from https://readingspark.wordpress.com/2019/06/19/picture-this-diversity-in-childrens-books-2018-infographic.*

It's unsettling that animals are more than two and a half times more present in children's books than Black people, almost four times more than Asian/Pacific Islander/Asian American people, five and a half times more than Latinx populations, and 27 times more than American Indians. A common argument is that animals are neutral and appeal to all children; however, when we think about the implications of that reasoning, what we find is deeply problematic. Children of color are regularly expected to—and do—read and enjoy literature and other media prominently featuring white characters, yet white children are rarely required to do so. The preference for "neutral" literature about animals indicates that white children feel more connected to, know more about, and identify more with animals than with other children simply because those children are of a different race. This sort of dehumanization of and lack of empathy for people of color is fodder for racist ideology. As Bishop (1990) puts it,

> Students from dominant social groups need to be able to look through the window of books to come to know people whose cultures are different from their own. If they only see reflections of themselves, they will grow up with an exaggerated view of their importance and value in the world—a dangerous ethnocentrism. (p. 7)

 The truth is that education is never neutral. We are complicit in oppression when we choose silence and erasure.

As teachers work to meet standards and provide quality literacy instruction, it could be easy to forget about incorporating diverse representation and perspectives into the curriculum; too often, culturally responsive teaching is considered an add-on or a separate curriculum (Souto-Manning, Llerena, Martell, Maguire, & Arce-Boardman, 2018). In truth, it's not culturally responsive if it's an afterthought or a stand-alone unit. Engaging in culturally responsive teaching requires constant reflection and awareness of how the instructional decisions you make *each day* are meeting the needs of *all* of your students and how you're providing both mirrors and windows to *all* students.

DISRUPTING THE SCENARIOS

So let's consider what that might look like in action in a primary classroom. In scenario 1, we met a teacher who used both whole- and small-group instruction to build phonological awareness with his kindergarten students. During whole-group instruction, he should be reading aloud texts that support this goal. That might include texts that rhyme and texts that include alliteration; however, when selecting those texts, he should also consider the following:

- Who is represented in my texts and how? Are diverse characters depicted in ways in which their diversity isn't central to the story (an important consideration for normalizing minoritized groups)? In contrast, are there also representations across the curriculum when their diversity *is* central to the story and I can highlight the mirrors/windows and have important conversations with students? Consider these examples:
  - *The Snowy Day* by Ezra Jack Keats is a book about a young Black boy who explores his neighborhood after a snowfall. Diversity isn't central

to the story, and we get to see a Black child living his everyday life. The text could support phonological awareness through a beginning sound search. After enjoying the book for pleasure, the teacher could reread the book, asking students to search for beginning /s/ sounds. For example, pages 9 to 10 read, "It was a stick—a stick that was just right for smacking a snow-covered tree."

- ○ *Islandborn* by Junot Díaz is a book about a young girl who learns about the island where she was born but does not remember through members of her family and community in the Bronx. <u>Diversity *is* central to the story</u>. The text allows us to expose children to immigration to the United States and island culture and to have conversations about both. Readers are exposed to a wide range of cultures from across the world from the perspective of children who have immigrated to the United States and specific information about the island that main character Lola is from. The text supports phonological awareness by offering another opportunity to notice alliterative beginning sounds. On page 3, the students are discussing the drawings they'll make of their first countries. "I'm going to put in pyramids," notes one student, and another says, "There's going to be a mongoose in mine."

- Who is silenced or minimized and how? Are certain people very obviously missing or relegated to the background? Is someone reduced to stereotypical depictions or contorted to socialized norms?
  - ○ *Prince & Knight* by Daniel Haack is a fairy tale in which a prince's parents search for a bride for him as he prepares to take the throne. Fairy tales typically promote gender norms and introduce the concept of sexuality and attraction to children at a very early age. In this rhyming tale, heteronormativity is counteracted when the prince falls in love with a knight instead. The villagers and the king and queen are all thrilled, and the text proclaims, "And on the two men's wedding day, the air filled with cheer and laughter, for the prince and his shining knight would live happily ever after" (p. 31). It's an excellent opportunity to normalize LGBTQ identities while addressing phonological awareness.
  - ○ *I Am Enough* by Grace Byers is a book about loving yourself and being kind to others. The illustrations feature a beautiful Black girl with lots of curly hair as well as children of different skin tones, abilities, and religions—children we don't see pictured as frequently as we should. The text's rhyme pattern supports phonological awareness and could easily be used as a precursor to practicing with common word families, such as "-ing." The text reads, "Like the sun, I am here to shine. Like the voice, I am here to sing. Like the bird, I am here to soar and fly high over everything" (pp. 4–5).

Remember, culturally responsive instruction is not one-size-fits-all. It might be easy to get pictures for phonics instruction from kits or Pinterest, but those images are not "neutral." They privilege white, middle-class, Christian norms like many other standard materials.

These books are not just for a certain time or subject. Using them during regular daily instruction normalizes diversity and sets a tone for an environment where everyone's identities are valid and belong in the curriculum.

Children's books are a wonderful starting point for ensuring representation, but the culturally responsive teaching is much bigger than book choices. Let's return to our scenario. Mr. Allen wisely uses picture sorts to give his students opportunities to practice their phonological and phonemic awareness skills in small groups. After whole-group instruction, small-group activity is a vital next step in gradually releasing responsibility to students as they move toward mastery and independence.

From a culturally responsive pedagogy lens, however, Mr. Allen should again reflect on his materials. His "neutral" pictures from the internet reflect mainstream cultural norms. Often, teachers understandably use what materials are readily available when they could instead take an (admittedly more time-consuming) opportunity to connect to students' lives. Instead, Mr. Allen could consider taking pictures of familiar items around the school and community. He might also intentionally search for (and of course teach children about) pictures that reflect a variety of cultures, as in figure 1.3.

CCSS.ELA-LITERACY.RF.K.2.A
Recognize and produce rhyming words.

hat   cat

Figure 1.3. Example Slide—Rethinking Images Used in Early Literacy Instruction.
https://www.pexels.com

Now let's consider the implications of this in scenario 2. Mrs. Travis has chosen books based on ensuring that she has a good mix of "boy books" and "girl books." To begin, how does she define "boy books" and "girl books"? To assign labels to books this way is problematic in that it sets up standards of who a boy or a girl is and what a boy or a girl enjoys or likes to do or cultural norms that are oppressive and constraining. Returning to the concepts of windows and mirrors, selecting texts that represent a range of gender identities, including nonconforming gender identities, allows possibilities for students to read about and connect to a wider range of conceptions about gender identities.

Next, Mrs. Travis has selected texts that fail to represent a range of diversity. Most of the covers of the books have characters that look alike (white) or animals. While the students in her class who are white and middle class might find themselves in these books, the remaining students will not. In addition, the majority of her students will fail to see windows of diverse representation and cultural experiences with these texts. It is important that even though many of the students are white and middle class in Mrs. Travis's class, she asks these students to examine diverse texts as windows and consider what they can learn about others and what they can learn about the world as well.

While text choice is important, Mrs. Travis should find a range of diverse books. If she is unsure how to find these resources, she can explore resources such as https://diversebooks.org, which focuses on "reflecting and honoring the lives of all young people," and http://americanindiansinchildrensliterature .net, which focuses on providing "critical perspectives and analysis of indigenous peoples in children's and young adult books." She can also find award-winning books that embrace Tricia Ebarvia, Lorena Germán, Julia Torres, and Kim Parker's notion to #DisruptTexts by disrupting the traditional canon and offering insights into real-world experiences of diverse people across different time periods and cultures, such as Rita Williams-Garcia's *Gone Crazy in Alabama*, Jacqueline Woodson's *Harbor Me*, or Jason Reynold's *Long Way Down*. Once she has found books that she might be interested in using for her novel units to represent mirrors and windows, she can assess these books with tools such as https://socialjusticebooks.org/guide-for-selecting -anti-bias-childrens-books and https://www.learningforjustice.org/sites/ default/files/2017-11/Reading-Diversity-v2-Redesign-WEB-Nov2017_0. pdf. These tools ask readers to critically reflect on the representation in texts and to pose questions related to cultural responsiveness as they choose meaningful texts for their classrooms.

Next, Mrs. Travis should consider how students can engage with the texts in ways that challenge their thinking, ask them to think critically, and help them examine the texts as both mirrors and windows. It is not likely that she is finding these types of questions in her multiple-choice downloads from the internet. Instead, she could be creating authentic tasks using formats such as choice boards with activities that connect home, school, and community or creating questions that, while also standards based, ask students to consider the assumptions the author makes, the voices that are amplified and missing, the impact of character identity on the events of the story, how students connect personally to the texts, and how characters enact agency. These questions can lead to thoughtful analysis about reading the world and connections to students and their lived experiences.

> Remember, culturally responsive instruction is not activities. Doing any of the following lessons without the requisite reflection and learning on your part is insufficient.

TWO LESSON EXAMPLES
FROM OUR LITERACY EDUCATION COURSES

What follows are two example lessons that take up the concepts of windows and mirrors in teaching materials to include culturally affirming and responsive literacy instruction. Each of the example lessons, as all of the example lessons in this book, have been created by us and recently taught in one of our university classrooms with our undergraduate students who are preservice teachers (PSTs) earning a license in K–12 reading education.

The first lesson, taught in Mikkaka's course on methods of primary reading, incorporates windows and mirrors by selecting a text that shows a young Black girl enjoying several things in her life to teach phonological awareness to early learners (K–2). The lesson, along with Mikkaka's implementation, demonstrates to readers how selecting a culturally responsive and affirming text is only one step in enacting culturally responsive pedagogy. Mikkaka provides a detailed description of how she models these lessons using this particular text to PSTs. What makes the example lesson different from the scenario with Mr. Allen is the way the lesson is connected to standards and to the lives of children.

The second example is a lesson that Christy teaches in her course on reading in a diverse world. Christy shares how she also utilizes the concept of windows and mirrors in the materials she selects and demonstrates how she teaches reading for social justice and action with her students. The lesson that Christy shares is focused on secondary students and combines a variety of texts that include diversity in communities and perspectives represented. What makes this example lesson different from Mrs. Travis's lesson is the focus on culturally responsive pedagogy with a diverse selection of texts and opportunities to center students in the learning process as they explore new perspectives and develop new knowledge both individually and with their peers.

> Remember, culturally responsive instruction is not one-size-fits-all. Before you use any aspects of these lessons in your classroom, remember to consider and reflect on your text.

Each of the two example lessons is presented to provide a glimpse into how we teach from a social justice perspective to enact culturally responsive literacy instruction in our teacher education courses. These lessons are meant to serve as examples of ways teachers can enact similar teaching stances with similar culturally responsive teacher moves in their own local context and with their own students. After the lessons, we provide guiding questions for readers to reflect about selecting materials for reading instruction considering the needs and interests of their own students.

ELEMENTARY LESSON EXAMPLE

One of my (Mikkaka's) favorite books to read aloud is _Honey I Love_ by Eloise Greenfield. The text has a joyful tone supported by its fun rhyming pattern as the main character recounts a list of things she loves. The unnamed main character is a carefree Black girl who enjoys a southern, African American lifestyle represented by activities like driving to the country "where the church folks like to meet" (p. 16) to eat and fellowship. For people like me, this is a mirror text, but for many of my students, it is a window into another culture.

I tend to read this book on the very first day of class and talk about the benefits of using it to build community (as well as a literate environment) at the start of the school year. There are many places in the text where a teacher might stop and allow discussion or use the pages as a writing invitation after a subsequent reading. For example, when the main character describes how she loves the way her cousin talks, I might invite PSTs to write about something they love about their family. I would be sure to describe family broadly to include and respect the many ways that can look for children.

After reading the book, I have PSTs "think like a K–2 student" and join me for circle time. I often ask them to move in and out of roles; sometimes, they think like teachers, and other times, I ask that they behave as children. In this example, I model as the teacher, and they engage with the activity as if they were children. We do a lightning share—everyone shares one thing they love or (as the main character in *Honey I Love* does toward the end of the book) one thing they do *not* love. I present this as an activity in which everyone can participate, including grumpy children, because there aren't correct answers and we can all contribute a like or dislike. Further, the PSTs are encouraged to snap their fingers in agreement if they connect to someone's like/dislike.

Continuing with the possibilities for extension activities related to this text, I suggest other quick community-building ideas that get kids moving. In "cross the room if," students stand in two lines facing one another on opposite sides of the room. The activity begins as teacher led, with the teacher calling out prompts like "cross the room if you love to read" or "cross the room if you do *not* love to sleep." The students who agree with the statement walk across the room to join the opposite line. (They're reminded that they don't have to talk; their movement or lack of movement speaks for them.) After the teacher prompts a few times, students are invited to take turns prompting.

Both of the previous activities serve multiple purposes. They provide an opportunity for students to get to know and connect with each other and for the teacher to learn more about the students as well. Of course, it's also a great brain break or movement break that doesn't take much preparation and can be as brief or lengthy as the teacher desires—perfect for a few unexpected minutes of downtime on the daily schedule.

After using *Honey I Love* for fun, it's sure to become a class favorite, so returning to it for further literacy instruction is engaging for students. Perhaps students have made heart-shaped collages or drawings, labeling things they love, or perhaps they decorate their name tents with the same information. For writing time, students can create their own minibooks that include several pages of their loves and one dislike, followed by the affirmation that concludes Greenfield's text: "And honey, I love ME too!"

Finally, the rhyme pattern used in this text makes it absolutely perfect for phonological awareness instruction. Rereading certain lines in the text during shared reading can be followed by working with students to meet CCSS. RF.K.2.A: "Recognize and produce rhyming words." With a big book or an enlarged copy of the text, students could be allowed to use highlighter tape (or highlight/underline on the smartboard or document camera if those tools are available) to identify the rhyming words in selected portions of the text. Then, as you move from recognizing to producing, perhaps you start with a shared writing experience. Consider the following:

Teacher: Today we are going to write about some of the things we love about our school. I have an idea to get us started. [read aloud as you write] I love going to this school. It helps me to be smart. I love the things we get to learn like reading, math, and _____? Hmm. What word might fit in the blank?

After reading the sentences again, students could be asked what word might sound right in the blank. If they're unsure, some turn and talk time might be useful before calling on individuals. In this pattern, the class could continue to write a poem together.

This whole-group practice could then move into small-group practice with rhyming words. Students could be provided frames to continue the class story, with various degrees of scaffolding (perhaps leaving more blank spaces or leaving the rhymes at the end of both phrases open for students to complete). They could alternately be provided with simpler frames to write their own poems. This also could move into word work with common rhymes, using familiar pictures as described earlier in this chapter.

> Remember, culturally responsive teaching is not "one more thing." These lessons aren't extra enrichment or for when you have "extra time." These lessons are to be integrated as a core part of your literacy instruction.

When I talk to my PSTs about all of this, I remind them of the importance of both the literacy and the culturally responsive pedagogy components of this lesson. While it's good practice to use quality literature and teach pho-nological awareness in context, it's also good practice to get to know your students and welcome and validate their home lives in your classroom. Books like *Honey I Love* provide opportunities to do both.

As your children grow to trust you and share aspects of their out-of-school lives with you, remember to accept and affirm the information they provide without passing judgment. Your instructional talk will be particularly impor-tant for this purpose, as we'll discuss more in chapter 3. Continue to reflect on your own experiences and biases and how that might influence the ways you perceive certain living situations, parenting choices, and families. The children in your room may represent families of a variety of races, religions, socioeconomic statuses, abilities, sexualities, and gender identities; regard-less of that fact, *all* of the families your students come from are valid and must be recognized as such. Different isn't "broken" or weird or sad. When you ask students to share who they are and where they come from, you owe them a safe space in which to do so.

Remember, culturally responsive instruction is not just for "those" kids. Considering your context doesn't mean that you reject these lesson ideas simply because you don't have Black or Muslim children in your class. White students like those whom our scenario's Mrs. Travis teaches need windows if we are going to build a more equitable society. A lesson like this one is valuable no matter the demographics of your classroom.

SECONDARY LESSON EXAMPLE

In the following lesson with PSTs who will teach secondary students, I (Christy) knew I wanted to both model and engage PSTs in how to meet the required standards, provide them an opportunity to examine multiple perspectives, and provide opportunities for critical thinking. In considering my goal of helping students view literacy through a social justice lens, I look to the discussion by Souto-Manning et al. (2018) of engaging students in social justice work. They suggest that in order to do this, teachers must "design learning experiences that allow students to unveil inequities" (p. 44). They also assert that in unveiling these inequities, students should engage in reflection and consider how they might interrupt injustice. With this in mind, I knew I needed to choose texts to both engage PSTs in the texts *as* students and *as* teachers and examine the texts in how they address diversity in authentic or in generic ways.

I chose two texts to explore the skills of two of our state standards: (1) examining texts from multiple perspectives and (2) comparing and contrasting texts. In addressing these standards, I also wanted to provide PSTs with an opportunity to consider the lives and experiences of others, using these texts as windows into the experiences of Sara Ahmed, at the time a college student living during September 11, 2001, and a fictional character, Maya, a Muslim American student living in the aftermath of this tragedy many years later. As mentioned earlier, these texts are representative of the richness and authenticity that #ownvoices authors bring to the world of literacy. With these texts, I wanted PSTs to examine their understandings of different cultures and consider the social justice implications of these two texts. I also wanted PSTs to see that texts by themselves are not culturally responsive but that how we ask our students to engage with these texts is how we create culturally responsive instruction.

In this lesson, I begin by reading three excerpts from Samira Ahmed's (2018c) *Love, Hate and Other Filters*. For each section, I ask students to ponder and write down any connections, thoughts, and questions they have related to the text. The first section I share is when the main character, Maya, is at school and she first learns there has been a terrorist attack. At this moment, many things go through Maya's mind, but her "absolute hope" is, "Please, please let everyone be okay. Please don't let it be a Muslim" (p. 145). From here, I go to a section where Maya discusses the attack with her parents. She is angry and sharing with her parents her frustration about how Muslims are perceived as "un-American and terrorist sympathizers. . . . It's guilt by association" (p. 155). In this exchange with her parents, Maya's father refers her back to her religion and discusses the Quran, reminding her that, based on their religion, it is a sin to take the life of innocent people, that "Terrorism has no religion. Think about Dylann Roof and that church in Charleston or the attack at the Sikh gurdwara in Wisconsin. Terrorists have their own ideology," he reminds her (p. 155). Finally, I share an excerpt of when Maya returns to school with her best friend after the attacks and runs into her classmate Brian. Brian taunts Maya, asking if the terrorist is her uncle because they share the same last name. In this exchange, Brian spews hatred toward Maya and Muslims in general, suggesting that if they don't like living in America, they should leave.

At the conclusion of this section, I provide final reflection writing time for students to write down connections, thoughts, and questions. I then ask students to share their responses with a partner. Once partners have shared their responses, I ask them to volunteer to share their responses with the whole class. By spending time sharing their responses with their peers, students become more confident in sharing their responses with the larger group. One student commented that he thought it was important that Ahmed referenced the Quran in the second excerpt and shed light on some of the beliefs described in the Quran. The student shared that this is often a misconception: when people think of Muslim terrorists, they often blame religion. This section of the text helped him see that the opposite is true. Another student shared that these excerpts helped her realize that when we look at marginalized people, "they feel the way they do, not because of who they are, but because of how we make them feel, how we treat them, how we respond to them." These responses to the reading were powerful in that PSTs were able to see new perspectives and examine and reconsider their beliefs and biases based on these perspectives. Through this text, we also explored questions about the author's purpose and how this purpose was conveyed throughout these excerpts. It was also important to discuss how the author positioned the main character, Maya. Who are her allies in the text? In the second excerpt, we see her friend stand up to Brian. I ask the students, "What would you do in this situation if you were Maya's best friend and Brian approached her this way? Would you be an upstander or a bystander?" (Ahmed, 2018b). How would you interrupt this injustice? We also discussed the role of the teacher in this text. Working with PSTs, I wanted them to consider how the teacher could have supported Maya.

Next, I moved on to the second text, which was a podcast by Sara Ahmed. In this podcast, Sara explains her immediate response and the aftermath of September 11 from a first-person perspective. I share the first part of this podcast, up to the point of Sara discussing the Transportation Security Administration pre-check. In this first section, Sara shares her initial responses, her fears, the role of her identity, and a conversation with her parents. Again, I asked students to reflect on this text, writing about their thoughts, connections, and questions. I ask the students to share these responses, first with a partner, then with the whole class. We discuss the author's message and also how the author chose to deliver this message. We discuss the impact of this medium on the message. PSTs responded that they could hear the "memory" in Sara's voice on the podcast, evoking emotion from the reader. The podcast, this firsthand account, allowed students to see briefly into the lived experience of Sara in this historical moment in time. As a class, we wrote about and discussed the similarities and differences in Sara's and Maya's experiences. We discussed the connections between the stories and characters as well as the role of the context (9/11 versus post-9/11). We discussed how Sara was a senior in college and Maya was in high school and how their identities and contexts may have influenced their actions. We also discussed the implications of the actions and inactions of the people around them.

An important point that arose during this conversation related to the context that even more than a decade later, connecting the past to the present in Maya's story, people still responded the same way, that even now, many people respond the same way to Muslims in America. While we explored similarities and differences and examined multiple perspectives in order to ensure that we were aligned to the required standards, we also studied the importance of examining our biases, questioning what we know, what we *think* we know, and what we do with this knowledge. The selection of these texts provided PSTs with the opportunity to examine the power of language in different mediums and from different perspectives as well as to make real-world connections to relevant texts. Finally, we also examined how to enact change when we see injustice. In choosing texts that included issues of inequity and injustice, I provided space for PSTs to examine resources they could use to help their students gain insights about important social issues of the past and present. The use of these texts also provided space for PSTs to think about how they might create spaces where their own students could gain a deeper understanding of the injustices in the world and consider how they might *act* on these injustices.

Throughout the lesson, I asked PSTs to consider how they could be agents of change as they encounter injustice. I asked them to sit with these texts as Ahmed (podcast) asked us as readers to do. At the conclusion of my lesson as the last PST packed up his belongings, he looked at me and said, "Dr. Howard, I'm not going to speak about the change, I'm going to *be* the change." Choosing materials that evoke these kinds of responses is how we can move our PSTs to explore literacy and learn through the lens of social justice as they consider how they might "interrupt injustice" within their lived experiences and help students do the same in their future classrooms.

CONCLUSION

As previously discussed, materials selection is an important piece of culturally responsive pedagogy. We hope in this chapter that you have noticed the diverse choices provided in these materials and the fact that these materials can be windows and mirrors for students that amplify the voices of diverse people and experiences. The scenarios provide insight into what we—and our teacher education students—often see and have experienced in K–12 classrooms.

As we reflect on these situations, we hope to disrupt the status quo in classrooms and in the real world as we provide lessons that ask our PSTs to critically reflect on social issues as well as their personal experiences. We also hope these lessons provide engaging and meaningful opportunities for PSTs as we acknowledge and validate their cultural experiences and help them see the cultural experiences of others. We intend for this disruption to build new knowledge and spark interests for our PSTs and our readers, to reflect and explore topics and ideas that interest them.

In lesson 1, we encourage you to pay special attention to how the selected text validates and accurately portrays aspects of southern Black culture and language patterns. As a literacy teaching exemplar, this lesson demonstrates how to use the gradual release of responsibility to scaffold instruction in phonological awareness. Simultaneously, it offers opportunities to get to know and build relationships with students so that you can build a truly affirming and inclusive environment in your classroom.

In lesson 2, we encourage you to pay special attention to the authentic, #ownvoices texts chosen. These texts are created by women with authentic connections and experiences that are reflected in these texts. In the tasks provided to PSTs, questions were posed that ask them to think of their personal responses to the texts, showing that their thoughts and voices are valued. Classroom spaces are created to question, think, and reflect on students' experiences reading the texts and their new learning as they individually and collectively grapple with the social issues presented.

This lesson not only provides a presentation of important social issues and appreciation of diverse perspectives but also leaves PSTs to question important teaching actions. As an educator, how could I have supported this student? What does it mean to be a bystander in this situation? What does it mean to be an upstander? How do my biases show up as a reader of this text? This is a lesson that allows PSTs to consider their role (both as K–12 student and as teacher) in these larger social issues and to begin to think of how they might positively enact change. The materials chosen for this lesson support this thinking and self-reflection, providing a tool to support social action and agency.

These lessons also provide an answer to the question teachers often ask: "How will I have the time to add something else to my curriculum?" Souto-Manning et al. (2018) remind us that we should not see culturally relevant instruction as an addition; instead, we should see it as an opportunity to reframe the prescribed curriculum. Choosing texts that are culturally responsive, including windows, mirrors, and #ownvoices texts, allowed for reframing literacy instruction and provided an opportunity to be "inclusive of historically marginalized and minoritized perspectives" (p. 39).

It is important to note that these lessons are starting points. Even if we shared all of our lessons, it is important to remember that culturally responsive pedagogy is more than creating meaningful lessons. It is an intentional way of thinking, it is a community, it is consistent practice, and it is commitment to culturally engaging and effective instruction. We hope that through these lessons, readers will take up the tenets of culturally responsive pedagogy and use these tenets to make decisions about materials in their own literacy teaching in their own classrooms with their unique students. As readers reflect on these lessons, we provide questions to ponder and continue the conversation in your own teaching context.

STOP AND REFLECT

- How can teachers teach curriculum standards using windows and mirrors materials?
- Consider the literacy standards for your grade level. Match these standards to windows and mirrors materials. Now fill in the blank(s) of what is missing based on the identities of your students.

- Consider the materials you usually use to teach an upcoming literacy topic. How can you incorporate materials that are more responsive, more relevant, and more affirming to all of your students?
- Create or use Interest Surveys so you can get to know what is important and culturally relevant to your students and their communities. Then use this information to choose and advocate for relevant materials in your classroom and school.
- Listen to community news or attend community events to find out more about student interests and/or relevant community topics. Then use this information to advocate for relevant resources and materials in your classroom and school.
- Create a text set using a collection of windows and mirrors texts that span across cultural groups. Then use the text set to teach a reading topic and related literacy standards.

Chapter Two

Instructional Language

Scenario 1

Mrs. Charles teaches at a grossly underfunded school. She is preparing her first graders to write personal narratives. After sharing a mentor text *The Relatives Came* by Cynthia Rylant (1993), Mrs. Charles gives the students a graphic organizer that features a child at the center of a thunderstorm thought bubble. Branching off from the child are numerous empty clouds. She starts with the following directions:

"Okay boys and girls, today we're going to begin thinking about our own personal narratives just like in the book. I want you to start by brainstorming ideas. Remember that these are true stories about interesting things that have happened to you. You can add more ideas tomorrow after you go home and talk to mom and dad."

Mrs. Charles comments on students' ideas as they work, sometimes to the whole class and sometimes just to individual students.

"Cheyenne is thinking of writing about the field trip to the zoo when she got to hold a boa constrictor. There are lots of details from that day that will make a good story!"

Mrs. Charles tries to coach Kameron: "Think about your favorite things to do at home," she coaxes.

He says, "I like going to the park with my moms."

Mrs. Charles straightens up to move on. "Okay, that's an idea. Go ahead and write that down, but keep thinking about things that would be exciting to read about."

Scenario 2

Mr. Goodrich teaches sixth-grade English at an affluent school in a suburb of a major city. His students are mostly white and upper middle class. Their parents regularly visit the school to volunteer, talk to teachers and staff, advocate for their children's needs, and attend school functions. The PTA offers lots of support, including raising money for events and providing each teacher an annual allotment of $500 for classroom supplies, and teachers can also request additional funding. The PTA votes on the requests, usually funding them in full.

Recently, Mr. Goodrich has noticed an increase in students using homophobic language. He's heard things like "that's so gay" and referring to certain male students as "sissy," "wuss," and "fag." He has decided to address the issue with the class. He begins a literature unit with "kindness" as the theme. He introduces students to the book they'll be reading, *Wonder* (Palacio, 2012).

"Boys and girls, we're going to start a new book today. I want to start by talking about the theme," he says. He turns to the smartboard and writes in large letters, KINDNESS. "Can anyone tell me what this word means?" Mr. Goodrich asks. Students give answers like "being nice" and "doing good things for people." When Mr. Goodrich asks for examples, students add "volunteering at the homeless shelter" and "giving Christmas presents to kids whose families can't afford gifts".

"Those are good examples," says Mr. Goodrich. "What about examples of everyday kindness? What about things you can do any day at school?"

There's a pause, and then a student volunteers, "You could sit with someone at lunch who is lonely and isn't, like, your normal group of friends. Or you can ask them to hang out or whatever."

"Those are good ideas. In our new book, *Wonder*, we'll meet a boy named August who needs that type of kindness. August gets bullied. Bullying is the opposite of kindness. Can you give me some examples of bullying?" The students reply that bullying includes calling people names, hitting people, giving wedgies, and putting kids' heads in the toilet.

"Does anyone here like being called names?" he asks. The students shake their heads. "August, doesn't either. People call him names because he's different. Do you think it's okay to call people names because they're different from you?"

Again the students shake their heads. Mr. Goodrich nods. "Of course not. We're all different in different ways, and that's okay. That's what makes the world interesting. We don't all have the same beliefs, and we don't all think the same way. We have different skin tones, heritages, languages, and abilities, but that's all good. In this classroom, we don't make fun of people because we think they're different from us."

With that, Mr. Goodrich begins handing out the books.

Instructional language is how teachers communicate ideas and concepts to students through their talk and through the language in the literacy materials they use for instruction. Peter Johnston has written two books about the power teachers have in the language they use in classroom literacy instruction. In his first book, *Choice Words* (2004), he shared examples of how well-intentioned phrases, such as "good job," can position students as capable or incapable literacy learners. In the example of "good job," Johnston wrote that when teachers use this phrase for some students and not for others, the implied message is that some students are doing well and other students are not. Those who do not hear "good job" about their learning can think they are doing a "bad job." Johnston makes clear that teachers being silent or omitting words can influence student identities and perceptions of selves as learners. Johnston continued his exploration of how teacher language works to position students and their identities as literate learners with his second book, *Opening Minds* (2012). In this book, he wrote, "Our language choices have serious consequences for children's learning and for who they become as individuals and as a community" (p. 7).

Although Johnston did not explore the connection between teacher language and culturally responsive instruction, the ideas and examples presented in his books lend themselves to our goals as culturally responsive teachers. First, Johnston is explicit about teachers having power in their language choices that influence how they teach students and how their beliefs about students are conveyed through these choices. Second, Johnston calls on teachers to be more aware of and intentional about the words that they choose during their literacy instruction. Finally, Johnston's attention to how teachers talk to, with, and about their students and to the lasting impacts on student identities and their positioning as capable or incapable learners is central to culturally responsive instruction.

As Johnston points out, the words and phrases we use or exclude in our instruction matters; whether we are introducing long vowel sounds in a primary phonics lesson or asking students about their reading comprehension of a text, the language we use as teachers makes visible our beliefs about teaching and our students, which translates into our instructional decisions and the materials we use. If our beliefs about teaching and our students stem from a deficit perspective, then we limit and restrict our students' identities as learners in our classrooms. In this chapter, we disrupt language that dismisses students' cultures and offer possibilities for teachers to affirm their students' identities and lives to ensure more equitable and culturally responsive instruction in K–12 classrooms.

In Candace Kuby's (2013) book about teaching for equity in a kindergarten summer program, she wrote, "Language is not neutral, and therefore the words teachers choose to use matter" (p. 95). Kuby elaborates on this idea throughout her book to investigate how the language she used to discuss social inequalities related to race was impacted by her beliefs and experiences as a white woman. Kuby shares her feelings of awkwardness and how her language evidenced these feelings through hedging statements, struggles for appropriate words, and using body language to fill in when affirming or accurate words were not readily available. Kuby's intentional reflection on and about her own language is a useful example to teachers as they become more aware of how their instructional language has consequences for their students' identities and conceptions of themselves as learners. Both Kuby and Johnston speak to the power of choice in the language that teachers use in their instruction and how being more metacognitive about words that are used impacts students beyond the instructional moment.

Being intentional and metacognitive about language choices is important; however, teachers may not be aware of how their identities and experiences impact their limited knowledge about topics or misconceptions they hold. Teachers may have to unlearn stereotypes, build their knowledge about topics that they have not yet explored, and evaluate their biases. One example may be LGBTQ-related topics, and, similar to the opening scenarios, teachers may avoid this topic if they hold misconceptions or biases or have limited knowledge about LGBTQ people and issues. Our preservice teachers (PSTs) share that they often feel unsure or uncomfortable with LGBTQ topics specifically and share that this uncertainty is related to perceived potential adult negative reactions or school policies that silence LGBTQ-inclusive curriculum.

Although these fears are unrelated to their actual experiences in schools, our PSTs are not alone. Jill Hermann-Wilmarth and Caitlin Ryan (2019), in their work with elementary teachers who implement LGTBQ-inclusive practices, found similar hesitations reported by teachers. However, as they have found in their years of research and countless professional development sessions, negative notions of parental or policy resistance can be interrupted when teachers learn more about LGBTQ topics and how to integrate more inclusive teaching practices into their curriculum and instructional decisions.

Teachers should engage in reflective work about topics they may hold misconceptions about or have little accurate knowledge of *before* they engage with students and families with these identities so that they are well prepared and accurately informed in their conversations. Take a few minutes to pause and consider the beliefs, experiences, and biases you may have begun to explore in chapter 1. Use these questions to guide you in reflecting about how they may influence your instructional talk:

- What topics might you consider taboo or inappropriate to discuss with students in your grade-level or classroom context?
- What questions might a student ask you about identities that you would not know how to answer in an accurate or affirming way?
- Where can you access more information about these topics to prepare yourself to welcome student questions, discuss topics using accurate language choices, and affirm students' inquiries?

• What topics are you "waiting to discuss" or learn more about only when you have students who identify this way?

DISRUPTING THE SCENARIOS

Now let's make more visible the places where our fictional teachers could have been more culturally responsive and affirm their students' experiences and cultures in their instructional language. In the first scenario, Mrs. Charles engages primary students in a very common literacy practice of using children's literature to generate student writing ideas and as a mentor text for writing in a specific genre. We applaud the concepts of reading aloud to students, students generating writing ideas from their lived experiences, and using a mentor text to structure genre writing; however, these instructional activities are not what we seek to disrupt in this section. Instead, we want to guide readers in how to make more deliberate culturally responsive language choices in their instruction to affirm their students' identities in their literacy instruction and curriculum.

In the first scenario, Mrs. Charles conveys multiple deficit perspectives about her students, their identities, and their experiences in her language choices. This stance positions some of her students as having limited or unimportant personal experiences and that they may be untruthful about their experiences. We see this perspective and positioning evidenced in the language choices Mrs. Charles makes throughout the scenario when she states that they will generate their own ideas "just like in the book" and that the brainstormed ideas must be "true" and "interesting" and include "good details." Mrs. Charles confirms this stance individually to Kameron when she omits "interesting" to describe his idea to write about going to the park with his moms and does not share his idea with the entire class. Instead of affirming Kameron's experiences or his ideas as worthy of being written in a personal narrative, Mrs. Charles's language choices position students like Cheyenne to have valid ideas by sharing Cheyenne's example with the entire class and using "interesting" to describe it.

Another belief Mrs. Charles conveys to her students is that personal experiences must be had with family, specifically, with mom and dad. Using these specific terms reinforces a belief that privileges gender binaries within heterosexual family structures and silences the range of family structures and gender identities that exist within her students' lives and in the community. Mrs. Charles demonstrates the belief about families through the text selection, *The Relatives Came* (Rylant, 1993), a story about a family reunion, and through her language choice of "mom and dad" and her quick reaction to

Kameron's topic of going to the park with his moms. How could Mrs. Charles make deliberate language choices to affirm her students' identities and position them as learners who can succeed in writing a personal narrative? The short answer is through knowledge about the topic of the lesson: her students' lives. The longer answer is in the following suggestions.

First, ensure that all students' personal lives are affirmed in classroom activities by continuing to get to know your students' identities and experiences, including family structure. Find out who your students live with at home through family surveys, conversations, or home visits, then affirm their families in your language choices. Be accurate in your language choices and avoid exclusionary terminology. Speak individually to students to affirm their family members and gender inclusiveness of their family members, that is, "mom(s)," "dad(s)," "grandparents," and so on. Also be sure to include nonbinary language to speak about family structures not represented in your students' lives and to provide windows into family structures unlike their own. A final suggestion is to use language that expands the genre of personal narrative beyond family experiences.

Since personal narratives can be about any experience students have had in their lives, teachers can affirm these experiences by selecting a text or a text set (a collection of texts about a single topic or theme) that provides mirrors for students. When introducing texts, teachers can choose affirming language to make more explicit the connections between students' experiences and the experiences in the text and point out how a personal narrative may be unique to the author. For example, Mrs. Charles can use the book *The Colors of Us* (Katz, 2002) and say to Kameron, "Look! This page reminds me of your experience of going to the park with your moms." A statement like this to each student both affirms their family experiences and positions them as writers of personal narratives.

Similar to the first scenario, Mr. Goodrich made sound instructional choices to select a young adult novel in which his students could find windows and mirrors at different points in the text; he also based his text selection on a general topic he wants his students to explore. However, like Mrs. Charles, Mr. Goodrich's instructional language should be disrupted to ensure more culturally responsive language choices that affirm his students' identities in his instructional practices and material selections.

The first belief that Mr. Goodrich demonstrates is that discussing homophobic slurs as a type of bullying is not appropriate in the classroom. This belief is evidenced when Mr. Goodrich avoids this topic and instead introduces a generic topic, "kindness," with the group novel, *Wonder*. This perspective is reinforced throughout the lesson in his language choices to discuss "examples of bullying" or "examples of kindness" unrelated to homophobia.

By ignoring homophobic slurs in his instruction, Mr. Goodrich dismisses the opportunity to build awareness and knowledge about LGBTQ people in his students' lives and in the world. Furthermore, by focusing on "kindness" as a general topic, Mr. Goodrich ignores the injustices experienced in LGBTQ communities when homophobic slurs are used. Avoidance of injustices and stereotypes of communities, including Auggie, the main character in *Wonder*, who is bullied and teased by his classmates because of his facial abnormality, allows misrepresentations and injustices to perpetuate. When educators "teach about love, acceptance and kindness without addressing inequit(ies), we gloss over crucial differences in the ways our students experience the world" (Turner, 2019, n.p.) and blatantly ignore identities and lived experiences of our students and their communities.

A bias that Mr. Goodrich enacts through language is equating "different" with "beliefs," "think the same way," and "skin tones, heritages, languages, and abilities" with bullying. What Mr. Goodrich implies through these choices is that his students are white and able-bodied and believe and think in similar ways. Justice is once again ignored for identities that do not fit within these confines and beliefs. Also, like Mrs. Charles, Mr. Goodrich used gendered language when addressing his students as "boys and girls," which highlights the misconception that all students fit within traditional gender identities of "boy" or "girl" and ignore nonbinary, genderqueer, or fluid identities. Although not explicitly mentioned in the opening scenario, we know from research and our own PST experiences that teachers can be worried about adult reactions to LGBTQ-inclusive materials and topics in schools. This may be the case for Mr. Goodrich, and we take issue with this belief because we know that many of these worries are unfounded, inaccurate, and exclusionary to families who identify as LGBTQ (Hermann-Wilmarth & Ryan, 2019).

Finally, Mr. Goodrich does not request funds to purchase books that center LGBTQ characters and experiences, though the PTA at Mr. Goodrich's school usually funds these types of requests. His decision to not request funds reinforces beliefs that LGBTQ topics are not appropriate in his classroom or school context and that the PTA would also share this belief. We advocate that educators who teach in schools where there is financial support and access to materials have an even greater responsibility to build their students' understanding and empathy about marginalized communities, such as LGBTQ people.

Suggestions for how Mr. Goodrich can be more aware of damaging language and make intentional choices to affirm student identities in instruction are similar to the suggestions made for Mrs. Charles. Both teachers can benefit from getting to know their students' lives and interests so that their identities and experiences may be affirmed in classroom instruction and language. Mr. Goodrich can be more deliberate about how he addresses students by using gender-neutral language, such as "students," or asking and using students' pronouns. A third suggestion for Mr. Goodrich is to locate resources, including *facilitative texts*, to learn more affirming and accurate LGBTQ vocabulary. Mr. Goodrich can use facilitative texts, which are texts that use accurate and positive language from the characters' perspective and identities (Howard & Ticknor, 2019), and additional resources in his literacy instruction. Facilitative texts and resources can be used to build knowledge about topics, affirming vocabulary, and historical context to address why these particular words are cruel and unjust.

EXAMPLES OF RESOURCES AND FACILITATIVE TEXTS FOR GENDER IDENTITY AND SEXUAL ORIENTATION

American Library Association. (n.d.). *Rainbow book list—GLBTQ books for children and teens.* https://glbtrt.ala.org/rainbowbooks

Learning for Justice. (n.d.). *The acronym and beyond.* https://www.learningfor justice.org/magazine/publications/best-practices-for-serving-lgbtq-students/ lgbtq-terms-definitions-the-acronym-and-beyond

Learning for Justice. (n.d.). *Section II: Classroom culture.* https://www .learningforjustice.org/magazine/publications/best-practices-for-serving -lgbtq-students/section-ii-classroom-culture

We Need Diverse Books. (n.d.). *Where to find diverse books.* https://diverse books.org/resources/where-to-find-diverse-books

Facilitative Text Examples:

Diloway, M. (2019). *Summer of a thousand pies.* New York: HarperCollins/ Balzer + Bray.

Emezi, A. (2019). *Pet.* New York: Make Me a World.

Gino, A. (2015). *George.* New York: Scholastic.

Haack, D. (2018). *Prince & knight* (S. Lewis, illus.). New York: Little Bee Books.

Hall, M. (2015). *Red: A crayon's story.* New York: Greenwillow Books.

Herthel, H., & Jennings, J. (2014). *I am Jazz* (S. McNichols, illus.). New York: Dial Books.

Hoffman, S., & Hoffman, I. (2019). *Jacob's room to choose* (C. Case, illus.). Washington, DC: Magination Press.

Holt, K. A. (2019). *Redwood and ponytail.* San Francisco, CA: Chronicle Books.

Howard, G. (2019). *The whispers.* New York: G. P. Putnam's Sons Books for Young Readers.

Howard, G. (2020). *Middle school's a drag, you better werk!* New York: G. P. Putnam's Sons Books for Young Readers.

Kilodavis, C. (2011). *My princess boy: A mom's story about a young boy who loves to dress up* (S. DeSimone, illus.). New York: Aladdin Books.

Lukoff, K. (2019). *When Aidan became a brother* (K. Juanita, illus.). New York: Lee & Low Books.

Nazemian, A. (2019). *Like a love story.* New York: Balzer + Bray.

Newman, L. (2009a). *Daddy, Papa, and me.* New York: Tricycle Press.

Newman, L. (2009b). *Mommy, Mama, and me.* New York: Tricycle Press.

Polacco, P. (2009). *In our mothers' house.* New York: Philomel Books.

Salazar, A. (2019). *The moon within.* New York: Arthur A. Levine Books.

Sanders, R. (2018). *Pride: The story of Harvey Milk and the rainbow flag* (S. Salerno, illus.). New York: Random House.

Slater, D. (2017). *The 57 bus: A true story of two teenagers and the crime that changed their lives.* New York: Farrar, Straus and Giroux.

Thomas, A. (2020). *Cemetery boys.* New York: Swoon Reads.

Woodson, J. (2010). *The house you pass by on the way.* New York: Puffin Books.

Finally, if Mr. Goodrich does know that his students' families would be concerned about inclusionary LGBTQ teaching practices, then we recommend that he talk directly with these families about the homophobic slurs he has overheard and explain the school's antibullying policy and federal antidiscriminatory guidelines. Instead of avoiding topics that may be perceived as controversial, we advocate for teachers educating themselves, their students, families, and communities about the injustices of discrimination.

TWO LESSON EXAMPLES
FROM OUR LITERACY EDUCATION COURSES

What follows in this section are two example lessons from our literacy courses highlighting instructional language that affirms student identities and positions students as literacy learners. Also included in each lesson are materials that provide both windows and mirrors for students (see chapter 2) and choice in student response (see chapter 4 for more details). These lessons are examples of the way we engage our PSTs in culturally responsive literacy instruction both as students and as future teachers. We do not offer these lessons as stand-alone, ready-to-implement lessons for teachers to use with their own students; rather, they are examples of how we scaffold our PSTs by modeling our own thinking to make deliberate language choices that affirm student identities and position students as literacy learners.

As we shared earlier, there are principles that guide our thinking, planning, and implementation of each lesson in this book. These principles guide the choices we make about the materials we select, the language we use, and the assignments we create. Each lesson is also influenced by who we are and what we believe about our students and teaching. Our individual identities inform how we make specific choices in our lessons; however, our decisions are guided by principles that we share collectively, outlined in chapter 1. Both of the following lessons were taught by Anne. In each lesson example, we share the lesson and make explicit the decisions about the language used in talk and in the literacy materials.

The first lesson taught is geared toward elementary-grade literacy instruction. This lesson uses Bishop's (1990) concept of windows and mirrors (chapter 2) to find texts about families. Anne models how to expand the definition of "family" by connecting the concept to students' individual families and then has students explore example texts about families to use in their future classrooms. The lesson includes using a story map to identify literary elements of a narrative text, which corresponds with CCSS.ELA-LITERACY.RL.1.3: "Describe characters, settings, and major events in a story," using key details; in addition, explicit examples of both using and scaffolding PSTs to use affirming and accurate instructional language is used throughout the lesson.

The second lesson is focused on secondary students, reading comprehension, and supporting comprehension with textual evidence. In this lesson, Anne modeled how to use dialogue journals to engage secondary students in writing and talking about books (CCSS.ELA-LITERACY.RL.8.6: "Analyze how differences in the points of view of the characters and the audience or reader [e.g., created through the use of dramatic irony] create such effects as suspense or humor" and CCSS.ELA-LITERACY.RL.8.1: "Cite the textual evidence that most strongly supports an analysis of what the text says explicitly as well as inferences drawn from the text"). Anne modeled this activity with her students and then modeled the thinking about how and why teaching decisions were made with specific attention to instructional language. The lesson illustrates Anne's use of affirming and accurate language with the specific topic of LGBTQ identities. Throughout both lessons, Anne shares examples of how she models her thinking about language and is explicit about how and why language choices are made.

ELEMENTARY EXAMPLE

I (Anne) introduce the theme of families, a typical topic in primary grades, as a mirror and window avenue to identify literary elements in a fictional text to my elementary education teacher education students. I tell them that I will model the process of a similar lesson with their future students and that I will pause at times to reflect on how I am engaging them both as students and as (future) teachers of children. I let students know that I want them to pay special attention to the language I am using in my talk with them and in the materials they use in the lesson.

I start the modeled lesson by asking them to spend a few minutes thinking about defining the concept of "family" and the members in their own families. After a few minutes of think time, I ask students to share with someone near them. Once they have shared, I ask for volunteers to share their definitions of family and the members of their families as I write responses on a T-chart with family definition on one side and members on the other side. Typically, students share definitions that include "the people I live with at home," "the people who raised me," or "the people I am related to." When asked about membership in families, students share "mom," "dad," "stepdad but really like my dad," "sisters," "dad's son lives with us," "grandma lived with us," "my uncle was living with us for a few months, so I guess he is family," "the friends I live with here are my family," and so on. As students share, I write what they say, and I revoice their responses. The reason I revoice is twofold: (1) I want to be sure I hear what they say, and (2) I want everyone else to hear the language their classmates are using to describe their families. I tell them that I am revoicing their responses for these reasons, and I tell them that by revoicing what your students say, it gives their responses credibility and gives them an opportunity to be the authority of who their family is. Once they stop sharing, I ask, "So what is a family? Who are the members of families?"

Remember, culturally responsive teaching isn't "one more thing." This lesson is an opportunity to teach traditional literacy skills in a thoughtful, affirming, and inclusive way. The choices you make in instructional talk, methods, and materials make all the difference.

The point of these questions is to have my teacher education students reflect on how the concept of family can be expanded to include several different structures and understandings. Students typically smile in response to my questions, some let out a small laugh, and others look away so I don't call on them. I then say, "So if in our class we have all of these different examples of what a family is and who the members are in our families, do you think your future students will have different concepts of families and memberships?" They nod in agreement, and I ask them to form small groups of five or six students to continue the modeled lesson.

I hand out a piece of copy paper to each person and show them how to fold it into four sections to create a story map, a strategy that uses a graphic organizer to record literary elements of a fictional text. I explain that our story map will have four elements central to fictional narrative texts: main character, supporting characters, setting, and problem with solution (CCSS. ELA-LITERACY.RL.1.3: "Describe characters, settings, and major events in a story, using key details" and CCSS.ELA-LITERACY.RL.1.7: "Use illustrations and details in a story to describe its characters, setting, or events"). We quickly review how to identify these elements in a narrative text, and I model where I would write these ideas on the paper. Then I hand out one book per group of several children's literature picture books that have a main character who is part of a family.

FAMILY TEXTS FOR BUILDING TEXT SET

Boelts, M. (2007). *Those shoes* (N. Z. Jones, illus.). Somerville, MA: Candlewick Press.

Bunting, E. (1991). *Fly away home* (R. Himler, illus.). Boston: Clarion Books.

Bunting, E. (1994). *Smoky night* (D. Diaz, illus.). New York: Voyager.

Cherry, M. A. (2019). *Hair love* (V. Harrison, illus.). New York: Kokila.

Choi, X. (2013). *The name jar.* New York: Knopf Books for Young Readers.

Cohn, D. (2002). *¡Si, se puede!/Yes, we can!* (F. Delgado, illus.). El Paso, TX: Cinco Puntos Press.

Cooper, M. (1998). *Gettin' through Thursday* (N. Bennett, illus.). New York: Lee & Low.

Cottin, M. (2006). *The black book of colors* (R. Faría, illus.; E. Amado, trans.). Toronto: Groundwood.

González, R. (2005). *Antonio's card/La tarjeta de Antonio* (C. C. Álvarez, illus.). San Francisco, CA: Children's Book Press.

Hazen, B. S. (1979). *Tight times* (T. S. Hyman, illus.). New York: Puffin Books.

Heide, F. P., & Gilliland, J. H. (1990). *The day of Ahmed's secret* (T. Lewin, illus.). Boston: Lothrop, Lee & Shepard.

Martinez-Neal, J. (2019). *Alma and how she got her name.* Somerville, MA: Candlewick Press.

Noble Mallaird, K. (2019). *Fry bread* (J. Martinez-Neal, illus.). New York: Roaring Brook Press.

Parr, T. (2003). *The family book.* Boston: Little, Brown.

Parr, T. (2007). *We belong together: A book about adoption and families.* Boston: Little, Brown.

Pérez, A. I. (2000). *My very own room/Mi propio cuartito* (M. C. Gonzalez, illus.). San Francisco, CA: Children's Book Press.

Quintero, I. (2019). *My papi has a motorcycle* (Z. Peña, illus.). New York: Kokila.

Woodson, J. (2002a). *Our Gracie aunt* (J. J. Muth, illus.). New York: Hyperion.

Woodson, J. (2002b). *Visiting day* (J. E. Ransome, illus.). New York: Scholastic.

Once all groups have a book, I say,

All of these books have a family in it; however, not all of the families have the same members in it. The reason I selected these books is to demonstrate a range of family structures, some of which were recorded in our T-chart, that may provide mirrors and windows for you and/or your future students. When you read the book with your group, pay attention to the four elements of the story map. Identify who the main character is and who the supporting characters are. Also, note the characters who are part of the family and their relationship to each other. Then identify the setting, the problem in the text, and the solution to the problem.

I give students time to read the book and complete the story map while I move around to each group to listen in, ask questions, or redirect as needed. My intention is to listen for, or scaffold, affirming and accurate language about families presented in the text. For example, I might say to a group who is not sure how to label the relationship of a supporting character, "How does the author describe the character in the book? What words or picture clues can you use from the text to describe their relationship?"

Once groups are finished, I tell them they will share what they learned about families represented in their book. Then we will talk across the books about families represented in the text set. Each group comes to the front of the room to share their book cover, title, author/illustrator, and story map. As each group shares, I again scaffold and affirm their language choices when describing the characters and the families in the book. I also remind the entire group of students to silently think about how each book shared may be a window or a mirror to themselves and/or their future students.

Once all groups have shared, I ask, "How many of you heard about a family like yours?" All students raise their hands. "How many of you saw a picture or illustration that looked like your family?" All hands raise again. Then I ask, "Did anyone not hear about or see their family represented?" No hands raise. "Would anyone like to share how it felt to see and/or hear your family represented in one of these books?" Students share their feelings, which tend to be positive. Every time I teach this lesson, at least one student shares that it was a realization that they had not seen their family represented in the books they read in elementary school because their parents divorced, a parent died, a parent was incarcerated, they have same gendered parents, they lived with their grandparents, and so on. After this statement, a few other students will nod and agree. Then I say,

> That must have hurt to not see your family represented. Now think about your future students. If we are not providing mirrors to all of our students that validate their lived experiences, then we are not positioning them as full members of our classroom community. If you know your students' lives, then you need to make every effort to be sure they feel seen in the curriculum you are teaching. You have that power, and that power can be exercised in the instructional materials you select and the language you use when you teach.

Then I ask students to spend a few minutes thinking individually about the misconceptions they may have had about families unlike their own. I say,

> Think about the books we just shared and think about the books that provided windows into a family structure you do not know. Now think about the misconceptions or stereotypes you may have had about this family structure before hearing about this book. What did you learn today that disrupted those ideas? Be thinking about the strengths of the family, the commonalities across all of the families in these books, and the words the main character used to describe their family in positive, strength-based ways.

After students think on their own, I ask them to share with their small groups. Then we share ideas aloud, and I write them down for all to see. I revoice their responses with attention to scaffolding and affirming strength-based language. Then I ask for any questions students may have about using a text set about families focused on inclusive representation of family structures or story maps with their future students. Finally, I share that books that provide both windows and mirrors for students about family structures should be used throughout the day in all literacy activities, such as read alouds, independent reading, guided reading, and shared reading, and as mentor texts for writing narrative texts and beyond.

SECONDARY EXAMPLE

I (Anne) begin this lesson in a similar way as the first lesson. I tell my teacher education students that I will be modeling a lesson that they may implement with their (future) secondary students to meet CCSS.ELA-LITERACY.RL.8.6: "Analyze how differences in the points of view of the characters and the audience or reader (e.g., created through the use of dramatic irony) create such effects as suspense or humor." I remind PSTs that one way to analyze differences in points of view is to ensure that a variety of perspectives are included so that students can compare and contrast a similar idea. For this lesson, I tell PSTs that we will read a variety of young adult novels centered around a common theme of pivotal moments in their lives. The text set includes novels with main characters from different identities who are all experiencing a pivotal moment in their life that impacts their identity significantly.

Then I book talk several young adult novels in a text set of books, including *The House You Pass by on the Way* (Woodson, 2010), *The 57 Bus* (Slater, 2017), *Dear Martin* (Stone, 2017), *A Time to Dance* (Venkatraman, 2014), *Indian No More* (Willing McManis, 2019), *Ghost Boys* (Rhodes, 2018), *The Hate U Give* (Thomas, 2017), *The Whispers* (Howard, 2019), *Clap When You Land* (Acevedo, 2020), *Long Way Down* (Reynolds, 2019), *Symptoms of Being Human* (Garvin, 2016), and *The Sword of Summer* (Riordan, 2015) (see figure 3.1). My intent in the book talks is to highlight the diverse identities of the main characters in each book. For example, in my book talk for *The House You Pass by on the Way*, I say,

> This is a book about a young girl, Staggerlee, who lives in the American South and is 14. Staggerlee feels "different" from her classmates and in particular from the other girls in her grade level. Her cousin, whom she has never met and is the same age, visits from Maryland to stay with her family for the summer. Staggerlee is excited to meet her cousin, Trout, because she thinks Trout might feel "different" too based on a picture of her. We quickly find out that part of why Staggerlee feels "different" from the other girls is because she is negotiating her identity and her sexual orientation, which is the attraction we feel toward another person. The pivotal moment for Staggerlee relates to the summer with Trout and the conversations they have about their identities.

After each book talk, I ask PSTs if they have any questions about the book. Often, PSTs ask questions about book characters with identities that are unlike their own or about language used in my book talks. For example, after introducing *The 57 Bus* (Slater, 2017), PSTs ask why I used the pronoun "they" to describe Sasha. I share,

> I use the pronoun "they" as a singular because that is the pronoun Sasha uses. Sasha explains how they came to use this pronoun very early in the book, and Sasha shares that they "didn't see themselves as fitting into neat either/or categories like male or female. Sasha, like many gender-nonconforming people, wants to be referred to with the pronoun *they*" (p. 15). I am respecting Sasha by using "they" when referring to Sasha.

I continue by explaining my decision making about why including novels with characters with diverse identities is important to include in a text set about point of view because it offers readers windows and mirrors into different perspectives:

> Point of view matters in who is telling their story and how that story is presented to an audience. If we only present one point of view then we—and our students—miss an opportunity to learn from a point of view that is a mirror to their experiences or a window. Secondary students, and even younger students, are trying to figure out their identities while you are teaching them, and you can support and affirm their identities by selecting literature that provides windows and mirrors into identities and perspectives about pivotal moments they may also be experiencing. These books and the language used by the characters provide you, as a teacher, an opportunity to welcome students' identities into your class and provides them an opportunity to see themselves in the curriculum you are teaching. You will notice that each of the main characters in the books have different identities, and the text set includes positive and affirming perspectives of LGBTQ people. This is important to include because your students are thinking about their identities in terms of gender and sexuality, which can be uncomfortable for teachers to acknowledge with their students.

I continue by pointing out how *The 57 Bus* (Slater, 2017) is particularly important because

> one of the reasons I purposefully select books like *The 57 Bus* (Slater, 2017) is because language is central to one of the main character's identity and Sasha is able to explain to readers why and how language is both inclusive and exclusive to people's identities. As Sasha explains, their identity was excluded in pronouns of "she" and "he" and included in the pronoun of "they." According to a recent study by the Trevor Project (2020), one in four LGBTQ youth (13 to 24 years old) use pronouns or pronoun combinations that fall outside of the binary construction of gender. Readers who have felt included by language, specifically pronouns, need windows into this experience to build understanding and acquire affirming language when referring to gender-nonconforming

people. Hearing Sasha explain in their own words is especially powerful, and as a literacy educator, it affirms the power that individuals have over language and their identities. This perspective and language is important for students to hear and learn so that they may acquire and use more inclusive language when referring to people in their lives and/or communities.

After sharing this information, I give PSTs a few minutes to consider and share ideas with their neighbors and ask follow-up questions. Usually, PSTs comment that they had not considered the importance of inclusive pronouns in books until hearing me explain it or sharing that they have a friend/relative who identifies as gender nonconforming and uses the pronoun "they." These follow-up comments affirm and extend my explanation.

Next, we return to the lesson process of ranking novel choices, forming same-book partnerships, and introducing dialogue journals as a reader response (see chapter 4 for more details about reader response), in this case for recording textual evidence to meet standard CCSS.ELA-LITERACY.RL.8.1: "Cite the textual evidence that most strongly supports an analysis of what the text says explicitly as well as inferences drawn from the text." PSTs will use the journals in their same-book partnerships and when they meet with different book partners to discuss point of view across thematic books. As PSTs meet with same-book partners, I circulate and listen in on their conversations.

Regardless of partner or small-group meetings, I listen in on discussions by moving between groups and scaffold affirming language, answer questions, or provide additional resources to explore and monitor both the act of being a student engaged in the lesson and a PST who may teach a similar lesson in the future. My goal is both to support PSTs learning how and why the literacy instruction is useful and to build affirming and accurate language so that they are comfortable talking about reading materials inclusive of LGBTQ identities with their future students, their families, and their colleagues. For example, when students are reading *The House You Pass by on the Way* (Woodson, 2010), they may have questions or misconceptions about the opening paragraph in chapter 2. Woodson writes, "She had kissed a girl once. In sixth grade. Hazel. She didn't remember how she and Hazel started being friends. . . . They had kissed after school one day, behind a patch of blue cornflowers" (p. 25). I would be sure to ask PSTs about their understanding of this scene, and in particular, I would ask if they had any questions about who "she" was in this chapter. If they were hesitant or had misconceptions in their responses, I would say,

This is Staggerlee (main character) remembering an important moment in her life two years earlier. Staggerlee's point of view is what we are learning in this scene that is pivotal to her life because she has told us how lonely she has felt in school and at home, that she feels "different" from her older sister and the other girls in her class. What makes this scene and memory so important is that she felt Hazel felt similar because she undid her hair when she was at school. This memory is also significant because she liked Hazel and wanted to continue being friends. Staggerlee is remembering this scene now because Tyler's picture reminds her of Hazel and Staggerlee is lonely and wants a friend who might feel like her: a bit different than the other girls she knows.

If PSTs were not sure how to describe Staggerlee's attraction to Hazel, I would scaffold their language by saying,

> At this point in the book, we do not know how Staggerlee identifies, and that is okay—this is Staggerlee's point of view, and we are learning from this character what she understands as a pivotal moment in a young person's life: a first kiss. She has not told us that she is a lesbian, that she is bisexual, that she is heterosexual, or that she identifies with another identity. It is okay because at this point we do not need to know, and it is also okay because Staggerlee, like many 14-year-olds, is trying to figure out who she is and whom she is attracted to. Not knowing adds to the suspense or drama about this story and the importance of trying to figure out love and attraction. Do you remember being 14 years old and thinking about who you were attracted to and how confusing it was sometimes? What I would encourage you to do is consider how your experiences and your identity might be a window into Staggerlee's experiences and/or how your experiences and your identity might be a mirror reflecting similarities to Staggerlee's experiences in this book. For me, a window in this text is that Staggerlee is attracted to Hazel, another girl, in this scene. Although this has not been my experience, the idea of being attracted to someone is a mirror because I have had that experience.

A final example of my instructional language is when same-book partners are meeting with partners who read a different yet similarly themed book. I try to affirm, scaffold, and provide additional resources as needed by particular groups and with all the groups. Before partners meet in small groups, I encourage all PSTs to listen to each other and try to find connections to the larger theme across the different books. I remind students of the overarching theme and that point of view creates such effects as suspense in telling pivotal moments in young adult characters' lives, and I encourage students to look for windows and mirrors between books and also their individual lives. When student partners reading *The House You Pass by on the Way* (Woodson, 2010) meet with partners reading *The Whispers* (Howard, 2019) their initial conversations usually start with identifying the main characters, their identities, and their point of view. This is important both to the theme of these books and to the Common Core Standards addressed in this lesson. One of the common themes in both books is that the main characters (Staggerlee and Riley, respectively) are trying to make sense of who they are and whom they are attracted to. In both texts, neither is clearly delineated by the book's conclusion; however, both convey similar messages: both characters feel "different" from the other kids, both characters have a sense of loneliness, and both characters find solace in nature. What is different in each book is that Staggerlee identifies as a girl and Riley identifies as a boy, which is important to point of view.

CONCLUSION

We began this chapter with two opening scenarios to provide insight into what we and our PSTs and in-service teachers may see in K–12 classrooms as examples to disrupt often well-intentioned but culturally dismissive instructional talk. How teachers use talk in their instruction conveys their beliefs about teaching and positions students in the learning activity. The intent of disrupting the scenarios is to focus readers on places where the fictional teacher should be more intentional and explicit in language choices to affirm students' lived experiences. The goal, then, of the example lessons is to provide literacy lesson examples with a specific focus on culturally responsive instructional talk that affirms students' identities and positions students as knowledgeable and capable learners.

In the first example lesson, we hope that readers learned how they too can disrupt limiting beliefs of family structure that silence their students' experiences outside of the classroom. We want readers to build their own knowledge and capitalize on the strengths of the diverse experiences of family that their students have. We also hope that students who see their families reflected in literature in the classroom are affirmed and that students who see families different than their own learn how to affirm these structures as well.

In the second lesson, our intent is for readers to use the text set as an example of how to include more inclusive texts into existing practices of reading comprehension and response instruction. The instructional language examples by Anne provide language and demonstrate how readers can be intentional about their language use in instruction that includes affirming and accurate language about identities and scaffolded conversations about text sets inclusive of LGBTQ characters. Our goal in this lesson is to affirm the identities in our classrooms and the identities of people in the larger community. We want readers to feel confident in how to normalize LGBTQ identities and language about identities in their literacy teaching and to disrupt the dominance of heterosexual lived experiences.

Both lessons highlight the use of facilitative texts and text sets that center around family structure and pivotal moments inclusive of LGBTQ experiences. It is important to note that both scenario school contexts included avoidance of LGBTQ identities. In the first scenario, Mrs. Charles dismissed

Kameron's lived experience of the park with his moms, and Mr. Goodrich avoids addressing homophobic slurs used by his students. The parallel between both contexts, an underfunded school and an overfunded school, is often not noticed as needing to center LGBTQ identities, which is not accurate. LGBTQ people and their identities exist in all spaces and communities.

When we teach these lessons to our teacher education students or during workshops with in-service teachers, we both model and highlight how we want them to talk with their K–12 students and the materials they use in their classrooms. Although these lessons focus on gender identity and sexual orientation, the format of both lessons could be used to include other identities as the central theme.

As a reminder, we do not offer either lesson (or any lessons in this book) as a one-size-fits-all lesson. We offer these as examples of how we teach PSTs and in-service teachers to be more metacognitive of their language, in both their instructional talk and the language in the texts they use for instruction, to be more inclusive and culturally responsive educators. Remember, culturally responsive instruction is an intentional way of thinking, an approach to planning instruction, and a lens through which to see all teacher–student interactions.

We hope in this chapter that you have not only noticed the ways that instructional talk is an important piece of culturally responsive pedagogy but also learned how to be more affirming in the language you use in instruction. To encourage you to stretch your thinking about developing more culturally responsive language, use the following questions to self-reflect and examine their own instructional language choices to affirm students' identities and position them as capable learners. Use these questions to ponder and continue the conversation in your own teaching context.

STOP AND REFLECT

- What words and phrases can you add to or remove from your instructional talk to position each student in your classroom as capable in every learning opportunity?
- How does your language affirm the identities of your students, their families, and the people they will meet in the community?
- What words and phrases can you add to or remove from your instructional talk to affirm each student's experiences and knowledge as valuable to their classroom learning?

Chapter Three

Reading Response

Scenario 1

Ms. Evans is a second-grade teacher. Her amazing group of students have many interests, including art, music, dance, writing, and sports. Ms. Evans's students are always eager to share what they are passionate about with her, and she enjoys sharing what she is passionate about with them: stories. Ms. Evans enjoys sharing stories with her students and sharing her favorite part of each story she reads with students. She also asks the students to share their favorite parts with her. She believes that this builds class community and that it will help students to enjoy reading. So today, as she finishes her read aloud of *Chrysanthemum* and closes the book, Ms. Evans asks students to return to their seats and take out their writing notebooks.

Ms. Evans is focusing on CCSS.RL.2.1. This standard requires students to "ask and answer such questions as who, what, where, when, why, and how to demonstrate understanding of key details in a text." In their writing notebooks, Ms. Evans asks students to complete a chart that addresses these standards by asking students to list who the story is about, what problem the character has to solve, where the story takes place, when the story takes place, and how the problem is solved. In addition to answering these questions, she wants to give them an opportunity to reflect on what they enjoyed about the text, so she posts a sentence stem on the smartboard—"My favorite part of the book was _____"— and asks students to complete the sentence to indicate their favorite part of the book and then to draw a picture. The students have many pictures in their writing notebooks representing the parts of the stories they enjoy. When Ms. Evans reads the students' writing notebooks, she sometimes makes comments about the similarities between the student's favorite part and her favorite part. While the students are working in their writing notebooks, Ms. Evans is choosing the story she will use tomorrow for this activity from her stack of favorite books.

Scenario 2

Mr. Lincoln's 10th grade English class has just finished reading a chapter in *The Great Gatsby*. During this unit, one of the standards he has been focused on is CCSS.RL.2.9-10. Part of this standard asks students to determine the theme of a text and analyze the development of the theme throughout the text. The standard also asks students to write an objective summary of a text. With this in mind, when Mr. Lincoln's students finish the chapter, he asks them to answer 10 multiple-choice questions about the text and then write an objective summary about what happened in the chapter. The students are asked to share their summary with a partner and make a prediction about what they think will happen in the next chapter. As they pair up, some of the students mention how they are tired of writing summaries for every chapter, and instead of discussing their summaries, they focus on socializing with their partner. Mr. Lincoln understands that the students are frustrated, but he feels he has to make sure they stay focused on the standard based on the pacing guide. As he plans his lessons for the following day, he looks for short stories to pair with the novel so that students can practice writing summaries about those texts too.

Often, K–12 teachers plan literacy lessons where a text is read, either by the teacher or by the student, then students are expected to respond to the reading. For many teachers, this is a daily or weekly activity, and they have learned that asking students to respond after reading helps students process the text in deeper ways. These teachers are right, and the practice should continue in classrooms; however, asking students to respond to a reading in the same way all the time through tasks such as multiple-choice questions, summaries, and drawing without providing space and avenues for students to choose how they represent and frame their responses to reading often discounts student knowledge and experiences, limits their responses, limits ownership in their learning, and devalues their culture.

Sometimes, teachers learn a new response strategy, and they are excited to use this strategy with all students. For example, when I (Christy) am teaching preservice teachers (PSTs) about a particular strategy, such as allowing students to showcase their learning through art and music, they ask, "What if all of your students don't like art or music?" My response is always to affirm that question with the fact that it is likely that all of their students won't like art or music, so let's provide them with choices. I suggest giving them some autonomy in their learning by considering the intended objective for the lesson and then considering the myriad ways students can arrive at those objectives.

Sometimes, teachers are afraid to give students choice and autonomy because they feel that it takes away their own control and can lead to behavior issues (Anderman & Mueller, 2010). However, the benefits should outweigh teachers' concern about control. Providing students choices in how they respond to texts can serve to both motivate and engage students (Anderman &

Mueller, 2010; Brophy, 2010; Eccles & Roeser, 2010). Additionally, teachers are often concerned about providing choices for students and still being able to meet the required standards and accountability measures (Amrein & Berliner, 2003). While many teachers are like Mr. Lincoln and recognize the importance of focusing on standards, it is important to understand that we can create culturally responsive learning experiences and give students ownership of their learning while addressing curriculum standards at the same time (Howard, 2016). This approach to teaching centers students and can motivate them in the learning process.

In addition to providing opportunities for students to choose how they respond to texts, it is also important that educators provide opportunities for students to respond to texts in ways that value and integrate the lived experiences of students. As we discuss throughout this book, it is critical that classroom teachers incorporate and affirm their students' cultures and real-world experiences into the context of their classrooms. We recognize that this approach may be complex for educators due to having different life and cultural experiences than their students.

As a young white woman who experienced life primarily in a small blue-collar town in the U.S. Midwest with life experiences including monolingual and primarily white spaces, Anne's move to North Las Vegas and teaching in a school where nearly 90 percent of students spoke Spanish as their first language made her cultural and lived experiences irrelevant to her students' lives. Anne quickly found that her "normalized" experiences were in the minority and that she held damaging assumptions and misconceptions about her students' lives. With support from mentors, her students, and their families, she learned how to disrupt her biases and limiting beliefs about teaching and her students so that she could make relevant and meaningful connections to her students' lived experiences and knowledge. Anne actively learned to recognize and affirm her students' knowledge by asking students about their lives, listening to their answers, and taking part in the community of the neighborhood school. Much in the same way Anne intentionally learned how to incorporate her elementary-age students' lives into their in-school literacy learning, we can provide similar opportunities for our PSTs in our literacy education classes to learn how to make their literacy instruction more inclusive for their future students.

In broad and general ways, we can teach our PSTs how to recognize and listen to the myriad ways K–12 students make sense of what they read and how they respond to reading. We do this through our intentional instructional practices of providing inclusive space for student voices and giving them the opportunity to make sense of texts beyond multiple-choice questions. We do this by creating opportunities for students to become critical consumers of texts as opposed to regurgitators of texts. We do this by considering what we want students to know about a text and by considering the funds of knowledge they bring into our classrooms that influence how they engage with a text.

Responses to reading should be an opportunity for students to showcase their knowledge and a way for educators to identify any misconceptions, but they should also be an opportunity for students to explore critical topics based on their own interests and findings. Responses to reading should provide an opportunity for students to share their learning and ideas and listen to the learning and ideas of their peers. As we create opportunities for students to respond to texts, we should consider the following:

- What does the text mean in the context of students' lived experiences?
- How can this meaning contribute to their understanding, critical analysis, and clarification of the text?
- How can this meaning push students' thinking further into new inquiry?
- Do these practices provide choices for students?
- Do these practices provide inclusive spaces for student voices?
- Do these practices meet the needs of all of our students?
- Are the ways in which students engage in responding to texts examples of equitable practices?
- Do the ways in which students respond to texts value the voices of students who have been historically marginalized? If not, how can we provide space for these voices as students respond to texts? How can we use reading responses to enact culturally responsive instruction?

DISRUPTING THE SCENARIOS

When we consider the importance of student choice, integrating the lived experiences of students, providing inclusive space for student voices, and providing opportunities for students to become critical consumers of texts, how do we evaluate the scenarios that introduced this chapter? In the first scenario, Ms. Evans reads to her students daily—an excellent practice—and every day, she asks them to reflect on the who, what, where, when, why of the text. After they address those key ideas and details (per CCSS.RL.2.1), they write about their favorite part of the text and draw a picture. As a former second-grade teacher, Mikkaka can remember the delight many students expressed when allowed to break out the crayons and markers with their writing notebooks. Perhaps Ms. Evans's students are similarly pleased and she takes pride in keeping them so happily engaged.

Unfortunately, students appear to be doing the same task each day, and this task does not involve much student choice beyond choosing their favorite part. While they do get to share in their writing notebooks, which Ms. Evans will read, they do not have the opportunity to share their favorite part of the story with their peers. Thus, their audience is somewhat inauthentic; it is simply a task to complete for their teacher. If it is for Ms. Evans's use only, then how is she using it? How is their writing being validated and meaningfully integrated into instruction? When Ms. Evans reads their responses, what does she hope to find? Does it inform her forthcoming book selections? Does it help her connect students with one another in ways that reflect or expand on their interests and experiences? Does it help her learn more about her students and thus inform other instructional decisions, delivery methods, materials selection, and her interactions with students and families?

In addition, Ms. Evans could ask students questions that require more critical thinking. What is her goal during the read aloud? How is it connected to a standard, objective, or other information she might want students to know? Does asking the students to complete a sentence and draw a picture address this goal? If so, once the students have achieved this goal, they should move on to another response strategy and, perhaps, another standard. Ms. Evans could provide different options for students to choose as they respond to the text. This could be as simple as a pocket chart with interchangeable sentence strips detailing the various response options for a given day (see table 3.1). These options should present opportunities for students to share their thinking and learning with their peers and share how their learning connects to their lived experiences.

Table 3.1. Primary Grade Reading Response Choice Examples

Answer the five Ws and share your favorite part of the story. Be sure to draw a picture! (RL.2.1)

Write a note to a friend recommending the book. Share key details but don't spoil the ending! (W.2.1)

Do a four-square diagram with words and pictures of the characters, settings, problem, and solution. (RL.2.7)

Do a compare/contrast. How is this story like and different from another story we've read? (RL.2.9)

Reflecting on Mr. Lincoln's lesson, students were asked to answer multiple-choice questions to assess their knowledge and then write a summary about the text. Mr. Lincoln has prioritized teaching the standards using texts suggested by his school district. There has long been a discussion around state and national standards when viewed through the lens of culturally responsive teaching. Often, teachers feel that they are unable to engage in culturally responsive teaching because they have to focus on their standards.

> Remember, culturally responsive teaching isn't "one more thing." You should be meeting teaching standards through culturally responsive teaching. In this case (and most others), more responsive and affirming methods actually make the lesson stronger and more engaging.

As educators, we have to realize that these two ideas do not have to be mutually exclusive. Teaching through a culturally responsive lens does not mean we are not addressing standards. If taught through a culturally responsive lens, the standards can provide opportunities for critical thinking, which is important. So we have to consider how our students can benefit from these standards in ways that are meaningful and engaging for them.

We can do this by using standards to guide our work with tasks that amplify, affirm, and validate the experience of students. While Mr. Lincoln is focusing on a particular standard, he is not asking his students to use this standard to engage in critical thinking. It has become a routine, and the students seem to be bored with it. The task is not relevant to their experiences, and they are not given any choice in how they will respond or share their knowledge.

As we consider how we can disrupt this scenario, there are many avenues Mr. Lincoln could take in making this task more culturally responsive. To begin, there are many opportunities for him to integrate choice. He could have given students a choice in the book they were reading. We do recognize that some texts are required in certain districts, but, if possible, he could have offered the choice of a more diverse novel that explores the American dream, such as *The Sun Is Also a Star* by Nicola Yoon (2016). If it was not possible to replace this text, Mr. Lincoln could have added supplemental choice texts in different genres, such as short stories, songs, or poetry, that might have been more relevant to the experiences of students. For example, he could have had students listen to music and analyze the lyrics or read the poem "I, Too" by Langston Hughes (1926). To bring a more critical lens to the text and to enhance the summary, Mr. Lincoln could have used one of these supplemental texts along with the required reading and provided the prompt "Summarize how the American dream is portrayed in this text compared to how it is portrayed in the Great Gatsby." To integrate the lived experiences of his students, Mr. Lincoln could have asked how these portrayals are similar to or different from the students' perspective of the American dream.

As we read this scenario about Mr. Lincoln, it is clear to us as readers that the students are not engaged in the task. Instead of answering multiple-choice questions and writing a general summary, Mr. Lincoln could have provided choices for reading responses that meet the standard related to determining and analyzing the theme and creating summaries. For example, he could have asked students to create a short podcast in interview style with a partner or individually. He could have asked them to create a multimodal project (a poem, a song, and so on) that summarizes the text and also addresses critical questions such as following: How does the time period impact each text? How would this story be different if it were set in the 2020s? How is the text connected to current social issues? What are the cultural norms in this text? How are they similar to or different from the cultural norms in your community?

These ideas are ways to disrupt the scenario by providing engaging opportunities for students to meet the lesson standards, to have a choice in how they meet the standards, and to feel that their voices and experiences are validated in the process. As we consider ways in which we want students to engage and respond with texts, we have to center their identities and their funds of knowledge, empowering them as learners. Meeting the standards is important, but we also have to consider how we can provide multiple pathways for students to do this.

Disrupting teaching by centering our students must be intentional work. It is not about creating lessons; rather, it is about the principles that guide the creation of the lessons. As we disrupt the scenarios above, it is not enough to identify the issues with each of the scenarios and suggest what each fictional teacher should have done to make the lesson more culturally relevant, but, as educators, we must enact intentional change ourselves. How do we put this disruption into our real-world practice? Knowing what to do is not enough: we must act.

TWO LESSON EXAMPLES
FROM OUR LITERACY EDUCATION COURSES

In this section, we explore two example lessons that provide opportunities for students to respond to texts with a focus on standards *and* with a focus on culturally affirming and responsive literacy instruction. In reviewing these lessons, it is important to understand that these are simply examples of how reading responses could look in classrooms. These are not one-size-fits-all approaches to teaching.

As you read these examples, it is important to look beyond the specific texts and tasks and consider the structures that are in place that allow for student engagement. What structures have the teachers created that provide choice? What structures provide opportunities for students' experiences to be valued and their voices to be affirmed? What structures are in place that give students the opportunity to be critical consumers of texts? How would this look in your classroom? Further, we invite you to examine the role of the teacher in these examples. As educators, what principles related to instructional practices must we hold? What understandings do we need to have about our educational systems?

In preparing classrooms to be culturally responsive and culturally affirming, educators have to understand that school was not originally designed for everyone. It was not built for everyone to find success. We see this when we examine traditional reading response tasks that provide a one-size-fits-all approach. We see this in reading response tasks where there is only one correct answer, and we see this in our educational system through high-stakes assessments. These are not contexts where marginalized students have traditionally found success because these are not contexts that were built with marginalized students in mind. As we think of creating spaces in our classrooms for all students to find success, it is important to consider how we can shift from traditional practices that value the dominant culture and consider how we can provide spaces for historically marginalized students to have their experiences and knowledge affirmed and valued in our classrooms.

These lessons provide a space for students to think critically about the texts they are reading and to make personal connections with the text not only in ways that extend their thinking but also in ways that make learning relevant to their lives. As with previous lessons we have shared, these example lessons have been created by us and taught in one of our university classrooms with our undergraduate students who are PSTs earning a license in K–12 reading education.

ELEMENTARY LESSON EXAMPLE

After a read aloud in a second-grade classroom, the teacher may ask students to draw a picture of a connection or disconnection to their own lives. For example, after reading aloud *Honey, I Love* (Greenfield, 2016), I (Mikkaka) had my PSTs create table tents with their preferred name, pronouns, and pictures of three to five things they love/don't love. We displayed these table tents throughout the semester to help me address my PSTs properly and to connect with their interests. After participating in the read aloud and lesson themselves, I suggested and discussed ways to use this book and lesson in K–5 classrooms. My suggestions included allowing students to orally share things they do/do not love, to write about their likes and dislikes, and to tailor movement and community-building activities to the text (see the elementary lesson example in chapter 2).

For this chapter on reading response strategies, this first lesson focuses on CCSS.R.L.2.4, "Describe how words and phrases (e.g., regular beats, alliteration, rhymes, repeated lines) supply rhythm and meaning in a story, poem, or song." I used this lesson at the end of the semester with my PSTs, but it can easily be used at the end of a unit or any time students might need a creative way to summarize an important topic.

To begin, I read *The Important Book* by Margaret Wise Brown (1949). This poetry book details the important aspects of various items using a predictable format. After reading the book, we explicitly discussed the book's format, specifically how the author used repeated lines to set the tone for the poem and to convey meaning. We noted how the first and final lines of the poem emphasized the main idea.

After this discussion, I asked my PSTs to respond to the reading by applying its format to their own reflections (see figure 3.1). Following the structure laid out in the text, PSTs wrote their own reflections on the important

The Important Thing About Teaching Reading

The important thing about <u>teaching reading</u> is that _____. It _____, and _____, and _____, and _____, and _____.But the important thing about <u>teaching reading</u> is that _____.

Figure 3.1. PST—The Important Book Reading Response Frame. *Original course materials developed by author Mikkaka Overstreet*

things about teaching reading. They then brainstormed ways they could use this strategy in their own classrooms. In addition to using the frame across subject areas to reflect on various topics, the PSTs thought the poems would be a fascinating way to allow students to introduce themselves and tell their teachers and classmates what is important about them.

At its simplest, using this frame as a reading response could allow students the freedom to choose what is most important about any particular text. Further, as a response to *The Important Book* itself, the frame offers an opportunity for students to choose what is important enough for them to write about, offering teachers a glimpse into their students' worlds. Imagine how much you could learn from this exercise about students' interests, families, and areas of expertise. Many books, such as *The Important Book* and *Honey, I Love*, offer excellent frameworks for tailored reading responses instead of cookie-cutter activities that aren't text specific.

SECONDARY LESSON EXAMPLE

This is a lesson, I (Christy) have modeled with my PSTs in a content area literacy course. The majority of PSTs in the course were history education majors, and this literacy course was intended to support their ability to integrate literacy into their high school history classrooms. This lesson could also just as easily be used in an English language arts class, as it addresses state and national literacy standards that focus on reading multiple texts, making inferences, and citing textual evidence.

For this particular lesson, I asked PSTs to respond to a set of texts focused on "freedom." The response tasks encourage their secondary students to engage with texts beyond retelling and push them to critically engage with each text. The three texts used were Langston Hughes's "I, Too" (1926), Franklin Delano Roosevelt's State of the Union Address (1941), and a photograph of the Olympians Black Power Salute (1968) (see table 3.2). Using multiple texts (poem, speech, and photograph) and giving secondary students multiple ways to respond to these texts helps us extend student comprehension beyond one text and one idea, allowing them to examine multiple ideas across texts as they analyze, synthesize, and evaluate information.

This lesson would take place over the course of several days because these are powerful, rich texts, and secondary students need to spend time exploring them as well as the context and systems that influence these texts. Each text is introduced individually, with the teacher providing contextual and historical information about each piece as needed. During this introduction phase, it will be important to front-load each text with discussions about the context of

Table 3.2. Freedom Text Set

Text	Initial Interaction with Text	Rationale
Franklin Delano Roosevelt's State of the Union Address (1941)	• Choose quotes that you would affirm and challenge (Brookfield & Preskill, 2006) • Discuss these quotes with your peers. Consider these questions in your discussion ○ What similarities do you see with your peers related to your affirmations? ○ What differences do you see? How are your challenges similar and different?	This task puts value on what the students see as important and asks them to critically consider what information they might challenge in a text based on their knowledge and experience. It also provides an opportunity for them to share and analyze their thinking with their peers, providing space for all voices.
Langston Hughes's "I, Too" (1926)	• Complete an analysis of the poem using the guiding questions below. ○ What is the author's message? ○ How does the author convey this message? ○ What is the mood of the poem? ○ How does the author convey this mood? ○ How does the author use language to provoke visual images?	While these questions are standards based, they also ask students to consider and examine the perspective of a Black man (the author) during a critical time in American history, and while this is based in a historical context, it may also be relevant to the lived experiences of students and real-world current events. The discussion of this text can provide an opportunity for students to make these connections.
Olympians Black Power Salute (1968)	Respond to the text by using a photo analysis tool from the national archives, https://www.archives.gov/files/education/lessons/worksheets/photo_analysis_worksheet.pdf	This tool asks students to critically analyze not only the photograph but also the context in which the photograph was taken with questions such as "What was happening at the time in history this photo was taken?" and "What other documents, photos, or historical evidence are you going to use to help you understand this event or topic?" In addition, this analysis tool provides space for students to engage in sourcing, corroborating, and contextualizing this document (Wineburg, Martin, & Monte-Sano, 2013).

the text or allow students time to research key highlights from the historical time period themselves.

Part I: During the initial interaction with each text, readers complete a response task.

Part II: Once each of the texts has been individually explored, responses have been completed, and the texts have been discussed as a whole class (over several days), readers are provided with the "Thinking across Texts" graphic organizer (see figure 3.2), which brings the texts together with the common theme of freedom, a theme that secondary students can easily relate to their lived experiences regardless of what those experiences are. Before seeing this organizer, students have had an opportunity to critically analyze and respond to each text through questioning, considering the perspectives of marginalized characters, and discussing their responses with their peers. This organizer gives them the opportunity to dig deeper into each text while also looking at similarities and differences across texts. At this stage, readers are also given the chance to choose a text with the theme of freedom. Their chosen text can be a poem, speech, video, song, and so on. They will use this chosen text to respond to the questions in the organizer.

This is an opportunity for readers to explore the texts as a group and to evaluate perspectives that may be different from their own and different from each other. With this in mind, readers are asked to view "freedom" from

	I, Too Sing America (1926) Langston Hughes	"State of the Union Address" (1941) Franklin Delano Roosevelt	*Olympians Black Power Salute* (1968)	Choice Text:
How is freedom represented in each text? Use evidence from each text to support your response.				
Do you think each author or subject (photo) believes they are free? Use evidence from each text to support your response.				
How does the time period of each text influence the idea of freedom? Use evidence from each text to support your response.				
How might this text be different if it were created today?				
What does freedom mean to you? How might your perspective of freedom compare to Hughes, Roosevelt and the Olympians?				

Figure 3.2. Thinking across Texts. *Original course materials developed by author Christy Howard*

the perspective of a president in a State of the Union Address, an African American poet in 1926, and athletes protesting at the Olympics. In addition, they are asked to view freedom from the perspective of the author or subject in their chosen text.

Part III: After responding to the questions in the graphic organizer, readers are asked to create two questions they would like to discuss in a whole-class seminar activity. At this point, readers have the opportunity to use the information they have gained through reading across texts and across multiple perspectives to create two questions of their own to share with the whole group in a discussion, giving them some choice and ownership connected to the larger discussion.

Giving secondary students ownership and choice with this task helps teachers see what students value. What do they want to share? What do they want to know? What thoughts are lingering after they have engaged with multiple texts? Their questions help us learn more about their thinking and their interests. They show us what is relevant to them and provide opportunities for us as educators to use their questions as a springboard for critical discussions. Combined, these tasks require critical analysis and engage the students as they reflect on their personal lived experiences, making learning relevant for them.

CONCLUSION

As teacher educators, we can demonstrate for PSTs how to access and affirm their future K–12 students' experiences and cultures to deepen learning by modeling culturally responsive literacy instruction in our teacher education courses. Through our modeling, we can call attention to literacy practices, such as reading responses, that may be well intentioned but irrelevant to students' cultures and lives. Teaching our PSTs how to disrupt culturally irrelevant (Souto-Manning, Llerena, Martell, Maguire, & Arce-Boardman, 2018) literacy instruction through meaningful response opportunities opens spaces for more inclusive literacy instructional practices.

Remember, culturally responsive teaching isn't activities. You have to engage in reflection, critical thinking, and growth. A lesson like this encourages the teacher *and* the students to expand their thinking—crucial steps to building a more equitable world.

In our work, we have had many teachers ask us how they can be culturally responsive to all students when all of their students are different. Engaging reading responses is one way to do this when we integrate student choice, provide opportunities to secondary students to engage as critical consumers of texts, value their lived experiences, and provide spaces for their rich, thoughtful voices in our classrooms. As students share their ideas, thoughts, and questions, they share what is relevant in their world.

Learning without the voices of our students is a biased, unbalanced approach, and we have to ask ourselves whether this is really even learning. As we think about creating culturally responsive classrooms, it is important in this process to be intentional. We must be deliberate as we consider the assignments we create for students, especially when we consider assignments related to how readers respond to texts. We want students to understand that in these responses, their voices are valued.

Yes, there will be answers that are correct, and there will be answers that are incorrect. However, as we explore different topics, issues, and texts within our classrooms, it is also important to value how readers come to these answers and how they realize that some answers will be less concrete, ambiguous, or situational, and in those times, their voices are just as important and validated. As previously mentioned, the reading responses themselves are not the point of this chapter; these responses may not be able to be replicated in your classroom. Instead, consider how they represent the intentional ways of thinking you must have as a teacher to implement these types of lessons and reading responses. Looking at this lesson, the focus of this design included the following:

- Choice
- Critical consumption and analysis of text
- Providing space to integrate the lived experiences of students
- Providing space to amplify student voices

These practices center students in the classroom. Consider how these practices might be enacted in your classroom.

As we consider the scenarios, the disruption, and the sample lessons, it is important to ask ourselves as educators whether we are creating safe, equitable, relevant spaces for our students. Do our students feel valued, supported, and empowered as they engage with and respond to texts? If we are not, what message does this send to them about what and who we value?

STOP AND REFLECT

- How can we ask students to respond to texts in a way that requires them to consider not only their perspectives but also the perspectives of others?
- How can we ask students to respond to texts in ways that ask them to connect and analyze critical real-world issues?
- As students respond to reading, are standards being met, *and* do students have an opportunity to showcase their thinking and learning in authentic, culturally relevant ways?
- How can we give students opportunities to connect their lived experiences to the tasks we create?
- Consider the ways in which you currently ask students to respond to texts. Write them down. Do these responses give students choice? Do these responses value and integrate the lived experiences of students? Do these responses provide space for student voices?
- What new ideas do you have for integrating reading responses in your classroom?

Chapter Four

Conclusion

When we first started writing this book, we knew our country was in a state of unrest (Kitch, 2018), and we knew that educators were interested in learning more of the how-tos in implementing culturally responsive pedagogy. Now that we are at the end of writing this book and our world is in a pandemic, our nation is crying out for justice for Black and Brown people, and our teachers have had to relearn how to teach while in remote spaces.

The police killings of Breonna Taylor and George Floyd propelled Americans to the streets to protest despite the pandemic. The collective outrage; calls for action from average people, celebrities, and politicians; and the overwhelming video evidence in these cases amplified a national conversation about racism. Now, antiracism is going the route of diversity, equity, and inclusion—everyone is talking about it. Universities and businesses have released antiracism statements. Black authors and books about race are topping the best-seller lists. Despite continued conservative resistance, many people seem ready to acknowledge and study the impacts of systemic racism and racialized oppression.

However, we know this is not enough. We have been on this precipice before. We have not forgotten the movement after Michael Brown was killed by police. Likewise, we haven't forgotten Freddie Gray, Sandra Bland, Philando Castille, Tamir Rice, and so many others. We haven't forgotten the shooting at the Pulse nightclub. We haven't forgotten this country's long history of turning away from hard truths and slipping back into "business as usual."

While many are fighting for equity, many others are fighting against it under the guise of patriotism. Former president Trump issued an executive order condemning critical race theory, restricting antiracist training, and implying that such work is racist and sexist toward white men (Trump, 2020). In a direct response to research about America's history of racial oppression presented in the 1619 Project (Pulitzer Center, n.d.), Trump proposed a new curriculum titled the 1776 Commission—a watered-down history of America that airbrushes our faults and whitewashes history worse than the biased way we've taught it for years. For too long, we've taught "the same colonized, sanitized, Eurocratic versions of history" (McCormack, 2020, p. 945), telling many of our students that the narratives of people like them were unimportant and didn't contribute to the body of knowledge worth studying. Now we face government interference that threatens to curtail the little progress we've made toward a more accurate and inclusive curriculum.

What happens after we read the books? What happens after the media stop covering the protests? What happens between one killing and the next hashtag? How do we stop a system of oppression that permeates every facet of our society?

We do not have the answers to these questions, but we hope that our book offers readers a chance to pause, critically reflect, and take action toward more culturally responsive literacy instruction in their K–12 classrooms. We intentionally framed this book within the context of literacy instruction because we believe (1) that literacy has been used historically as a means to either elevate or marginalize certain voices, communities, and people and thus is particularly in need of a social justice and equity–oriented restructuring and (2) that literacy instruction lends itself naturally to culturally responsive instruction because of the freedom it offers teachers to select materials and methods. We advocate that readers disrupt their literacy instruction to include more culturally responsive and affirming practices and materials into their day-to-day teaching *right now*—not tomorrow, not when "*that* student/ parent/family" enrolls, not when the political climate changes, not when the violence against Black, Brown, and LGBTQ people stops. Your students are *already waiting* for you to lead. They are *already looking* to you and to the other adults in their lives to share your identities, listen to them talk, and write about what matters in their lives and to use this knowledge to make your teaching more responsive and affirming *right now*.

As we have shared, this work does not end. This is a continual and recursive process of intentionally thinking about how educators can make more culturally responsive and affirming decisions in their literacy instruction. We, too, continue to critically reflect on our own identities and grow in our own culturally responsive teaching. We, too, know how difficult this work is and how important it is to have educators who are committed to working together call each other out, share our failures, celebrate our growth, and engage in the sometimes difficult conversations. We know that teaching requires learning how to sit with discomfort and push ourselves beyond our complacency so that we can better support and affirm our students. One example of our continued growth and pushing ourselves happened when we were writing chapter 3 for this book.

We knew that identities would be central to a chapter about instructional language and how educators can engage in conversations that accurately affirm a wide range of identities in the classroom and beyond, specifically sexuality, sexual orientation, and gender identities. We knew that LGBTQ identity was a topic that some of our preservice teachers (PSTs) and in-service teachers felt hesitant discussing in the classroom. We also knew that research has shown that other educators share this sentiment (Ryan & Hermann-Wilmarth, 2019) and that teachers often have misconceptions about parents' reactions to LGBTQ topics in elementary classrooms. Ryan and Hermann-Wilmarth found that most parents are appreciative of teachers' inclusion of LGBTQ identities and that *if* parents had hesitations, one area was curriculum and lesson planning. For these reasons, we wanted our readers to be more confident in their instructional language inclusive of LGBTQ identities in their curriculum.

Anne was lead author on this chapter, and her goal was to normalize affirming and accurate language related to LGBTQ identities. She wanted to provide readers with examples of real language that she uses when talking with PSTs, teachers, and K–12 students. As shared in chapter 1, Anne was confident in her support of adults who identified as LGBTQ, but she was not prepared to enact support or affirmation of her elementary-age students who identify as LGBTQ. Anne hadn't yet read the research about children identifying their gender around ages 2 to 3 (Rafferty, 2018) or that adolescents typically understand their sexual orientation around age 10 (Institute of Medicine, 2011). Throughout the years since then, Anne has learned more about the research on these topics and learned in personal ways how to be an ally and an advocate for people who identify as LGBTQ. Going into the drafting of the chapter, we knew that Anne would write the lessons because she taught very similarly themed lessons in our collaborative research study of teaching PSTs culturally responsive pedagogy. What we did not know is how our funds of knowledge and identities would interact with the lessons and in the conversation that occurred during our chapter draft review.

Because we wrote much of this book during the pandemic, when we discussed this chapter and gave feedback, we were on a video call. The conversation became intense as we discussed each of our levels of comfort with the lessons and how each of our identities and experiences with students informed our perspectives. We found out quickly that each of us was coming to the lessons with biases about love, sex, sexual orientation, and gender identities. This was one of the most difficult conversations we had as a writing team, as colleagues, and as friends. It was awkward, it was scary, it was real, and it occurred in an online conference. If we had not done the work of building trust of and support with each other early in our relationship, our conversation may not have been productive and this book not completed.

Because each of us comes to culturally responsive pedagogy with our own identities and our unique experiences, we must continually reflect critically about who we are and what we believe about teaching and our students. This is a process that does not end when approaching teaching through a culturally responsive lens. The above example of one of our more recent ones of how having a group of trusted colleagues is essential to supporting this type of reflection. If you do not yet have a group of coconspirators (Love, 2019), you can build one through educating yourself about your biases and finding people whom you can trust to help you navigate that process so that you can become a more culturally responsive teacher who is ready to position students as allies and advocates who are already knowledgeable and curious.

On its website, the United Nations Educational, Scientific and Cultural Organization (UNESCO) calls literacy a "human right, a tool of personal empowerment and a means for social and human development." Further, UNESCO acknowledges that the definition of literacy is shrouded in political, social, and economic theories (Overstreet, 2018; UNESCO, 2005). As Mikkaka has written previously (Overstreet, 2018),

> At its most basic level, literacy can be defined as the ability to read and write (and, perhaps, to speak and listen), but these skills cannot be separated from the larger contexts of society that require individuals to use literacy as a means to communicate, interact, learn, and acquire power (Keefe & Copeland, 2011; Perry, 2012; UNESCO, 2005). Powerful literacy enables people to attain individual freedoms and a better understanding of the world. (UNESCO, 2005)

As culturally responsive teachers committed to equitable practice, we want to ensure that we prepare PSTs to see the connection between literacy, liberation, and power. Consequently, this book demonstrates how we can give all students access to powerful, liberating literacy in our classrooms. In her discussion of liberation and power in education, bell hooks (1994) asserts "the classroom should be a space where we're all in power in different ways" (p. 152). She suggests that students leave our classrooms "with a sense of engagement, with a sense of themselves as critical thinkers" (p. 158). The lessons in this book demonstrate this notion of teaching and learning. We do not believe that culturally responsive instruction exists without liberatory practices, and this belief is seen in our guiding principles. Collectively, these principles and our lessons call for engagement, inclusive learning, and critical thinking, which align with hooks's (1994) discussion of liberatory practices.

GUIDING PRINCIPLES

- *Culturally responsive instruction is not one-size-fits-all.* By definition, this type of instruction is contingent on context. You cannot and should not pick up the lesson examples in this book and deliver them directly to your students. You must make considerations for the unique contexts in which you teach and learn and instead take up the principles guiding this work.
- *Culturally responsive instruction is not activities.* One cannot simply do our suggested activities and consider their instruction to be culturally responsive. You must also "do the work." This means changing your ways of thinking about teaching and students, engaging in deep reflection and committing to a lifelong learning process of staying current on appropriate and affirming language choices, issues of equity, and societal trends.
- *Culturally responsive instruction is not just for "those" kids.* This is for everyone. All of our students deserve to be properly prepared to live in a diverse world. Affirming their cultures does not mean that you teach this way only if you have "diverse" kids in your classroom. For starters, diversity is far more than what you can see, so you must expand your thinking. Further, this work requires a disruption of traditional teaching, which is rooted in white, cisgender, Christian, abled, heteronormative, middle-class ideals. This has to be done in *all* classrooms so that *all* children can see themselves *and* others as a valid and valued part of the curriculum.
- *Culturally responsive instruction is not "one more thing."* This isn't an add-on or one more entry on teachers' already long to-do lists. Culturally responsive teaching is a method, a lens, or a frame through which all of your teaching passes. You don't set aside a block of time for culturally responsive teaching; rather, you do it all day. Math, literacy, science, social studies, art, physical education, music, and all other subjects can and should be taught in culturally responsive ways and with a culturally responsive intentional way of thinking.

In each chapter, we provided a view into classrooms where literacy is liberation, where, through the lessons, students are engaged as critical thinkers and are not dominated and controlled by our beliefs as educators. Instead, they are given relevant texts to explore and choose from along with opportunities to thoughtfully engage with their peers and instructors around ideas and social issues that are meaningful to them. Opposed to scripted cookie-cutter lessons, we provide guiding principles that represent a way of thinking about the importance of culturally responsive instruction. These lessons provide opportunities for inquiry and critical thinking where teachers can feel they are meeting the expectations of required standards and students can feel the freedom to learn these standards through choices in texts, content, and tasks. Further, the lessons in this book show that we believe that liberation is about acting—it is about exploring identity, agency, and social action. By giving K–12 students ownership to explore topics that are meaningful to them and asking them to take a critical lens to texts by examining representation, the notion of justice, and inequity, we teach them how to be social actors in the world. We teach them that they have the ability to enact change and that literacy is a tool that can help them in this process.

In many schools, particularly in schools that serve marginalized students, literacy is not connected to freedom. Instead, it is connected to scripted curriculum guides with a focus on isolated skills that promote "teach to the test" tasks. This approach to teaching not only limits learning but also denies access to culturally responsive instruction and critical thinking. This approach does not ask K–12 students to think about freedom and justice in their communities, and when we limit access to these aspects of learning, we fail to validate the brilliance and excellence that our students bring to the classroom (Muhammad, 2020). In doing this, we send the message that students' stories and voices do not matter. We stifle who they are rather than engage them in liberatory literacy practices that foster and validate what brings them joy and what they may seek to change. In addition, we fail to provide K–12 students with tools that will help them navigate the world outside of our classrooms. In this book, we ask our readers to examine their instruction. Does your instruction limit liberation, or does it promote liberation? Does your instruction show students how to be change agents and upstanders? Does it show students how to be critical thinkers for themselves, or does it show students how to regurgitate what you want them to know?

We pose these questions because it is important to reflect on the classroom culture we create. It can be easy to get lost in the required curriculum and texts, and we recognize that sometimes we are not given options about what to teach. However, when we think about helping students navigate the world, we have to consider how we can disrupt the scripted, cookie-cutter approach and make learning meaningful and relevant for every student in our classroom. The guiding principles in this book help us do this through a culturally responsive lens. We live in an imperfect world where racism, bias, and hatred exists. We have to continue to teach our students that they can make a difference in the world by being upstanders and change agents. Teaching literacy as a liberatory practice can help them on this journey.

Through this book, we hope we have shown our readers ways to engage students in meaningful literacy instruction, and it is our hope that this book is a resource to help our readers embrace culturally responsive teaching as a way to bring equity and freedom into classrooms and into the world. We hope that you have discovered new ideas for exploring your identity and the identity of your students. We hope that you have ideas for how to confront damaging talk about students by educating yourself about misconceptions, stereotypes, and biases. We hope that this book gives you ideas for helping students respond to texts and for choosing texts for your classroom. We also hope that you use this book as one part of your learning process and that you continue to expand your ways of thinking and learning about culturally responsive instruction through other resources as well. These are our ideas, based on our experiences, and we are excited to share them with you. Every day, we are learning more about ourselves and our students through this important work. We are learning more about how to collaborate and learn from others so that we can be better equipped for the ways in which our world continues to change, and this is just one part of our journey.

To the teachers, teacher educators, PSTs, and other education professionals who have made it this far, thank you. We truly hope that what you've found in these pages has been helpful, thought provoking, and inspiring. We believe in teachers. We believe that you came to this book with a breadth of knowledge and skills that we could build on. We believe that you were prepared to push your practice farther. We know that all educators are lifelong learners, and we are grateful to share the journey with you.

Bibliography

Acevedo, E. (2020). *Clap when you land.* New York: Quill Tree Books.

Adichie, C. N. (2009). *The danger of a single story* [Video speech]. http://www.ted.com/talks/chimamanda_adichie_the_danger_of_a_single_story.html

Ahmed, S. (2018a, September 12). *Being the change, a story* [Audio podcast episode]. https://blog.heinemann.com/sara-ahmed-on-identity-and-experience

Ahmed, S. (2018b). *Being the change: Lessons and strategies to teach social comprehension.* Portsmouth, NH: Heinemann.

Ahmed, Samira. (2018). *Love, hate, and other filters.* New York: Soho Press.

American Library Association. (n.d.). *Rainbow book list—GLBTQ books for children & teens.* https://glbtrt.ala.org/rainbowbooks

Amrein, A. L., & Berliner, D. C. (2003). The effects of high stakes testing on student motivation and learning. *Educational Leadership, 60*(5), 32–38.

Anderman, E. M., & Mueller, C. E. (2010). Middle school transitions and adolescent development. In J. Meece & J. S. Eccles (Eds.), *Handbook of research on schools, schooling, and human development* (pp. 198–215). New York: Routledge.

Angelou, M. (1984). *I know why the caged bird sings.* Boston: Little, Brown.

Babbitt, N. (2007). *Tuck everlasting.* New York: Square Fish.

Bishop, R. S. (1990). Mirrors, windows, and sliding glass doors. *Perspectives: Choosing and Using Books for the Classroom, 6*(3), ix–xi.

Bissonnette, J. D. (2016). The trouble with niceness: How a preference for pleasantry sabotages culturally responsive teacher preparation. *Journal of Language and Literacy Education, 12*(2), 9–32.

Boelts, M. (2007). *Those shoes* (N. Z. Jones, illus.). Somerville, MA: Candlewick Press.

Brookfield, S. D., & Preskill, S. (2016). *The discussion book: 50 great ways to get people talking.* San Francisco, CA: Jossey-Bass.

Brophy, J. E. (2010). *Motivating students to learn.* London: Routledge.

Brown, M. W. (1949). *The important book.* New York: Harper & Brothers.

Bunting, E. (1991). *Fly away home* (R. Himler, illus.). Boston: Clarion Books.

Bunting, E. (1994). *Smoky night* (D. Diaz, illus.). New York: Voyager.

Byers, G. (2018). *I am enough* (K. Bobo, illus.). New York: Balzer + Bray.

Cherry, M. A. (2019). *Hair love*. (V. Harrison, illus.). New York: Kokila.

Choi, X. (2013). *The name jar.* New York: Knopf Books for Young Readers.

Cohn, D. (2002). *¡Si, se puede!/Yes, we can!* (F. Delgado, illus.). El Paso, TX: Cinco Puntos Press.

Colfer, C. (2012). *The wishing spell*. Boston: Little, Brown.

Common Core State Standards Initiative. (2010). *Common core standards for ELA and literacy in history/social studies, science, and technical subjects.* Washington, DC: National Governors Association/Council of Chief State School Officers.

Cooper, M. (1998). *Gettin' through Thursday* (N. Bennett, illus.). New York: Lee & Low Books.

Cottin, M. (2006). *The black book of colors* (R. Faría, illus.; E. Amado, trans.). Toronto: Groundwood.

Darling-Hammond, L. (2008). Teacher learning that supports student learning. *Teaching for Intelligence, 2*(1), 91–100.

Díaz, J. (2018). *Islandborn* (L. Espinosa, illus.). New York: Penguin Young Readers Group.

Diloway, M. (2019). *Summer of a thousand pies.* New York: Balzer + Bray.

Duyvis, C. (n.d.). #ownvoices. https://www.corinneduyvis.net/ownvoices

Dyches, J., & Boyd, A. (2017). Foregrounding equity in teacher education: Toward a model of social justice pedagogical and content knowledge. *Journal of Teacher Education, 68*(5), 476–490.

Eccles, J. S., & Roeser, R.W. (2010). An ecological view of schools and development. In J. Meece & J. S. Eccles (Eds.), *Handbook of research on schools, schooling and human development* (pp. 6–21). London: Routledge.

Emdin, C. (2016). *For white folks who teach in the hood . . . and the rest of y'all too: Reality pedagogy and urban education.* Boston: Beacon Press.

Emezi, A. (2019). *Pet.* New York: Make Me a World.

Garvin, J. (2016). *Symptoms of being human*. New York: HarperCollins.

Gay, G. (2010). *Culturally responsive teaching: Theory, research, and practice* (2nd ed.). New York: Teachers College Press.

Gay, G. (2013). Teaching to and through cultural diversity. *Curriculum Inquiry, 43*(1), 48–70.

Gay, G. (2018). *Culturally responsive teaching: Theory, research, and practice* (3rd ed.). New York: Teachers College Press.

Gino, A. (2015). *George.* New York: Scholastic.

González, R. (2005). *Antonio's card/La tarjeta de Antonio* (C. C. Álvarez, illus.). San Francisco, CA: Children's Book Press.

Greene, B. (1974). *Phillip Hall likes me, I reckon maybe.* New York: Puffin Books.

Greenfield, E. (2016). *Honey, I love* (J. S. Gilcrest, illus.). New York: HarperCollins.

Haack, D. (2018). *Prince & knight* (S. Lewis, illus.). New York: Little Bee Books.

Hall, M. (2015). *Red: A crayon's story.* New York: Greenwillow Books.

Hamilton, V. (1974). *M. C. Higgins the great.* New York: Simon & Schuster Books for Young Readers.

Hazen, B. S. (1979). *Tight times* (T. S. Hyman, illus.). New York: Puffin Books.

Heide, F. P., & Gilliland, J. H. (1990). *The day of Ahmed's secret* (T. Lewin, illus.). Boston: Lothrop, Lee & Shepard.

Henry, O. (1906). The gift of the magi. In *The four million*. New York: Doubleday, Page & Company.

Hermann-Wilmarth, J. M., & Ryan, C. L. (2019). Navigating parental resistance: Learning from responses of LGBTQ-inclusive elementary school teachers. *Theory Into Practice, 58*(1), 89–98.

Herthel, H., & Jennings, J. (2014). *I am Jazz* (S. McNichols, illus.). New York: Dial Books.

Hoffman, S., & Hoffman, I. (2019). *Jacob's room to choose* (C. Case, illus.). Washington, DC: Magination Press.

Holt, K. A. (2019). *Redwood and ponytail*. San Francisco, CA: Chronicle Books.

hooks, b. (1994). *Teaching to transgress: Education as the practice of freedom*. London: Routledge.

Howard, C. (2016). Engaging minds in the common core: Integrating standards for student engagement. *The Clearing House: A Journal of Educational Strategies, Issues and Ideas, 89*(2), 47–53.

Howard, C. M., Overstreet, M. H., & Ticknor, A. S. (2018). Engaging preservice teachers with culturally responsive pedagogy: Three model lessons for teacher educators. *Journal of Language and Literacy Education, 14*(2), 1–19.

Howard, C. M., & Ticknor, A. S. (2019). Affirming cultures, communities and experiences: Teaching for social justice in teacher education literacy courses. *The Clearing House: A Journal of Educational Strategies, Issues and Ideas, 92*(1–2), 28–38.

Howard, G. (2019). *The whispers*. New York: G. P. Putnam's Sons Books for Young Readers.

Howard, G. (2020). *Middle school's a drag, you better werk!* New York: G. P. Putnam's Sons Books for Young Readers.

Hughes, L. (1926). I, too. In *The weary blues*. New York: Knopf.

Huyck, D., & Dahlen, S. P. (2019, June 19). *Diversity in children's books 2018*. https://readingspark.wordpress.com/2019/06/19/picture-this-diversity-in-child rens-books-2018-infographic

Institute of Medicine, Committee on Lesbian, Gay, Bisexual, and Transgender Health Issues and Research Gaps and Opportunities. (2011). *The health of lesbian, gay, bisexual, and transgender people: Building a foundation for better understanding*. Washington, DC: National Academies Press.

Jimenez, L. M. (n.d.). Booktoss: No easy book love. https://booktoss.org

Jimenez, L. M. (2014). So, like, what now? Making identity visible for preservice teachers. *Journal of Language and Literacy Education, 10*(2), 69-86.

Johnston, P. H. (2004). *Choice words: How our language affects children's learning*. Portsmouth, NH: Stenhouse Publishers.

Johnston, P. H. (2012). *Opening minds: Using language to change lives*. Portsmouth, NH: Stenhouse Publishers.

Jones, S. P. (2020). Ending curriculum violence: Yes, curriculum can be violent—whether you intend it or not. Here's what it looks like and how you can avoid it. *Teaching Tolerance Magazine.* https://www.tolerance.org/magazine/spring-2020/ending-curriculum-violence

Katz, K. (2002). *The colors of us.* New York: Square Fish.

Keats, E. J. (1976). *The snowy day.* New York: Penguin Books.

Keefe, E. B., & Copeland, S. R. (2011). What is literacy? The power of a definition. *Research and Practice for Persons with Severe Disabilities, 36*(3–4), 92–99. https://doi.org/10.2511/027494811800824507

Kilodavis, C. (2011). *My princess boy: A mom's story about a young boy who loves to dress up.* (S. DeSimone, illus.). New York: Aladdin Books.

Kitch, S. (2018). Feminist tweets to Trump: How to find commonality in diversity. *Taboo: The Journal of Culture and Education, 17*(2), 10–35. https://doi.org/10.31390/taboo.17.2.05

Kuby, C. (2013). *Critical literacy in the early childhood classroom: Unpacking histories, unlearning privilege.* New York: Teachers College Press.

Ladson-Billings, G. (1995). But that's just good teaching! The case for culturally relevant pedagogy. *Theory Into Practice, 34*(3), 159–165.

Ladson-Billings, G. (2000). Fighting for our lives: Preparing teachers to teach African American students. *Journal of Teacher Education, 51*(3), 206–214.

Laman, T. T., Miller, E. T., & López-Robertson, J. (2012). Noticing and naming as social practice: Examining the relevance of a contextualized field-based early childhood literacy methods course. *Journal of Early Childhood Teacher Education, 33*(1), 3–18.

Lewis, C. S. (1994). *The lion, the witch, and the wardrobe.* New York: HarperCollins.

Love, B. (2019). *We want to do more than survive: Abolitionist teaching and the pursuit of educational freedom.* Boston: Beacon Press.

Lukoff, K. (2019). *When Aidan became a brother* (K. Juanita, illus.). New York: Lee & Low Books.

Martinez-Neal, J. (2019). *Alma and how she got her name.* Somerville, MA: Candlewick Press.

McCarthey, S. J., & Moje, E. B. (2002). Identity matters. *Reading Research Quarterly, 37*(2), 228–238.

McCormack, S. (2020). Backpack of whiteness: Releasing the weight to free myself and my students. *Urban Education, 55*(6), 937–962. https://doi.org/10.1177/0042085919892035

Moll, L. C., Amanti, C., Neff, D., & Gonzalez, N. (1992). Funds of knowledge for teaching: Using a qualitative approach to connect homes and classrooms. *Theory Into Practice, 31*(2), 132–141.

Muhammad, G. (2020). *Cultivating genius: An equity framework for culturally and historically responsive literacy.* New York: Scholastic.

Muhammad, I. (with Ali, S. K.). (2019). *The proudest blue: A story of hijab and family* (H. Aly, illus.). Boston: Little, Brown Books for Young Readers.

National Center for Education Statistics. (2016). *Enrollment and percentage distribution of enrollment in public elementary and secondary schools, by race/ethnicity*

and region: Selected years, fall 1995 through fall 2024 [Data file]. https://nces
.ed.gov/programs/digest/d14/tables/dt14_203.50.asp

Nazemian, A. (2019). *Like a love story.* New York: Balzer + Bray.

Newman, L. (2009a). *Daddy, Papa, and me.* New York: Tricycle Press.

Newman, L. (2009b). *Mommy, Mama, and me.* New York: Tricycle Press.

Nieto, S., & Bode, P. (2012). *Affirming diversity: The sociopolitical context of multi-
cultural education.* Boston: Pearson.

Noble Mallaird, K. (2029). *Fry bread* (J. Martinez-Neal, illus.). New York: Roaring
Brook Press.

Olympians black power salute (1968) [Photograph]. https://www.history.com/
news/1968-mexico-city-olympics-black-power-protest-backlash

Overstreet, M. (2018). All work and no play makes Jack a dull boy: The case for play
at all educational levels. *Reading Psychology, 39*(2), 216–226. https://doi.org/10.1
080/02702711.2017.1415240

Palacio, R. J. (2012). *Wonder.* New York: Knopf.

Paris, D., & Alim, H. S. (Eds.). (2017). *Culturally sustaining pedagogies: Teaching
and learning for justice in a changing world.* New York: Teachers College Press.

Parr, M., & Campbell, T. A. (2011). Educating for identity: Problematizing and de-
constructing our literacy pasts. *Alberta Journal of Educational Research, 57*(3),
337–348.

Parr, T. (2003). *The family book.* Boston: Little, Brown.

Parr, T. (2007). *We belong together: A book about adoption and families.* Boston:
Little, Brown.

Paulson, G. (1988). *Hatchet.* New York: Trumpet Club.

Pérez, A. I. (2000). *My very own room/Mi propio cuartito* (M. C. Gonzalez, illus.).
San Francisco, CA: Children's Book Press.

Perry, K. (2012). What is literacy? A critical overview of sociocultural perspectives. *Journal of Language and Literacy Education, 8*(1), 50–71. https://eric
.ed.gov/?id=EJ1008156

Polacco, P. (2009). *In our mothers' house.* New York: Philomel Books.

Pulitzer Center. (n.d.). *The 1619 project curriculum.* https://pulitzercenter.org/lesson-
plan-grouping/1619-project-curriculum

Quintero, I. (2019). *My papi has a motorcycle* (Z. Peña, illus.). New York: Kokila.

Rafferty, J. (2018, September 18). *Gender identity development in children.* https://
www.healthychildren.org/English/ages-stages/gradeschool/Pages/Gender-Identity
-and-Gender-Confusion-In-Children.aspx

Reese, D., & Mendoza, J. (Eds.). (n.d.). American Indians in children's literature.
https://americanindiansinchildrensliterature.blogspot.com

Reynolds, J. (2019). *Long way down.* New York: Caitlyn Dlouhy Books.

Rhodes, J. P. (2018). *Ghost boys.* Boston: Little, Brown Books for Young Readers.

Riordan, R. (2006). *The lightning thief.* New York: Penguin.

Riordan, R. (2015). *The sword of summer.* New York: Disney Hyperion.

Roosevelt, F. D. (1941, January 6). *State of the union address.* https://millercenter.org/
the-presidency/presidential-speeches/january-6-1941-state-union-four-freedoms

Ryan, C., & Hermann-Wilmarth, J. (2018). *Reading the rainbow: LGBTQ-inclusive literacy instruction in the elementary classroom.* New York: Teachers College Press.

Rylant, C. (1993). *The relatives came* (S. Gammell, illus.). New York: Aladdin Paperbacks.

Salazar, A. (2019). *The moon within.* New York: Arthur A. Levine Books.

Sanders, R. (2018). *Pride: The story of Harvey Milk and the rainbow flag* (S. Salerno, illus.). New York: Random House.

Slater, D. (2017). *The 57 bus: A true story of two teenagers and the crime that changed their lives.* New York: Farrar, Straus and Giroux.

Snicket, L. (1999). *The bad beginning: Or, orphans!* New York: HarperTrophy.

Souto-Manning, M., Llerena, C. L., Martell, J., Maguire, A. S., & Arce-Boardman, A. (2018). *No more culturally irrelevant teaching.* Portsmouth, NH: Heinemann.

Stone, N. (2017). *Dear Martin.* New York: Crown Books for Young Readers.

Taylor, M. (1976). *Roll of thunder, hear my cry.* New York: Puffin Books.

Thomas, A. (2017). *The hate u give.* New York: Balzer + Bray.

Thomas, A. (2020). *Cemetery boys.* New York: Swoon Reads.

Ticknor, A. S., Overstreet, M., & Howard, C. M. (2020). Disruptive teaching: Centering equity and diversity in literacy pedagogical practices. *Reading Horizons: A Journal of Literacy and Language Arts, 59*(1). https://scholarworks.wmich.edu/reading_horizons/vol59/iss1/2

Trevor Project. (2020). *Research brief: Pronouns usage among LGBTQ youth.* https://www.thetrevorproject.org/2020/07/29/research-brief-pronouns-usage-among-lgbtq-youth

Trump, D. (2020, September 22). *Executive order on combating race and sex stereotyping.* https://www.whitehouse.gov/presidential-actions/executive-order-combating-race-sex-stereotyping

Turner, B. (2019). Teaching kindness isn't enough: Teaching kindness is a staple of elementary practice, but that isn't the same as teaching justice. *Teaching Tolerance Magazine.* https://www.tolerance.org/magazine/fall-2019/teaching-kindness-isnt-enough

United Nations Educational, Scientific and Cultural Organization (UNESCO). (2005). *Education for all: Literacy for life.* Paris: UNESCO.

U.S. Department of Education Office of Planning, Evaluation and Policy Development, Policy and Program Studies Service. (2016). *The state of racial diversity in the educator workforce.* https://www2.ed.gov/rschstat/eval/highered/racial-diversity/state-racial-diversity-workforce.pdf

Venkatraman, P. (2014). *A time to dance.* New York: Penguin.

Villegas, A. M., & Lucas, T. (2007). The culturally responsive teacher. *Educational Leadership, 64*(6), 28–33.

We Need Diverse Books. (n.d.). *Where to find diverse books.* https://diversebooks.org/resources/where-to-find-diverse-books

Williams-Garcia, R. (2016). *Gone crazy in Alabama.* New York: Armistad.

Willing McManis, C. (with Sorel, T.). (2019). *Indian no more.* New York: Tu Books.

Wineburg, S., Martin, D., & Monte-Sano, C. (2013). *Reading like a historian: Teaching literacy in middle and high school classrooms*. New York: Teachers College Press.

Woodson, J. (2002a). *Our Gracie aunt* (J. J. Muth, illus.). New York: Hyperion.

Woodson, J. (2002b). *Visiting day* (J. E. Ransome, illus.). New York: Scholastic.

Woodson, J. (2010). *The house you pass by on the way*. New York: Puffin Books.

Woodson, J. (2018). *Harbor me*. New York: Nancy Paulsen Books.

Yoon, N. (2016). *The sun is also a star*. New York: Random House Children's Books.

Zoss, M., Holbrook, T., McGrail, E., & Albers, P. (2014). Knotty articulations: Preservice teacher reflections of teaching literacy in urban schools. *English Education, 47*(1), 33–68. http://cccc.ncte.org/library/NCTEFiles/Resources/Journals/EE/0471-oct2014/EE0471Knotty.pdf

Index

Page references for figures appear in italic.

About the Authors

Anne Swenson Ticknor is associate professor of literacy studies at East Carolina University. She teaches graduate- and undergraduate-level literacy education courses with a focus on social justice and equity. She has more than 20 years of experience as an elementary teacher, professional development facilitator, literacy specialist, and teacher educator. Ticknor researches the topics of identity, relationships, agency, and learning as mediated through literacy. In addition to these topics, she publishes and presents nationally and internationally on single-story representations of historical events in children's literature, identity negotiation in personal and professional spaces, diversity and equity in literacy education, and relationships within communities of learners. Ticknor has received several awards and honors recognizing her focus on diversity, inclusion, and mentoring new faculty.

Christy Howard is associate professor of literacy studies at East Carolina University, where she teaches undergraduate and graduate courses. She believes that students should have access to teachers who believe in affirming and validating their experiences. This is evident in her commitment to teaching through a social justice lens. Prior to becoming a professor, Howard served as a middle school English language arts classroom teacher, an English language arts curriculum specialist, and an instructional support coach. Through her research and service, she continues to serve teachers throughout the state. Howard's research, teaching, and service focus on content area literacy instruction, culturally responsive pedagogy, and teacher preparation. She is the recipient of multiple teaching and diversity awards from East Carolina University.

Mikkaka Overstreet has been an educator since 2006, earning her PhD in curriculum and instruction in 2015. She was an elementary teacher for five years, then a literacy consultant for the Kentucky Department of Education. After earning her PhD, Overstreet returned to her alma mater, the University of Louisville, to serve as a clinical professor and director of the Minority Teacher Recruitment Project. Currently, she is assistant professor of literacy studies at East Carolina University. Her research focuses on exploring intersections of literacy, identity, and learning, particularly related to culturally responsive pedagogy. Her recent publications include in the *Journal of Language and Literacy Education*, the *NASPA Journal about Women and Gender in Higher Education*, *College Teaching*, and *Reading Horizons*. You can learn more about Overstreet on her website, www.drmikkaka.com. You can also find her on Facebook, Instagram, and Twitter under the handle @drmikkaka.

Made in the USA
Coppell, TX
21 January 2022

71995630R00062